DATE DUE

	DISCARDED		

A M E R I C A N
P R O F I L E S

NINETEENTH-CENTURY WRITERS

■

Steven Otfinoski

Facts On File
New York • Oxford

Nineteeth-Century Writers

Copyright © 1991 by Steven Otfinoski

Facts On File, Inc.   Facts On File Limited
460 Park Avenue South   Collins Street
New York NY 10016   Oxford OX4 1XJ
USA   United Kingdom

Library of Congress Cataloging-in-Publication Data
Otfinoski, Steven.
   Ninetenth century writers / Steven Otfinoski.
     p.   cm. — (American profiles)
   Includes biographical references and index.
   Summary: Contains profiles of ten nineteenth—century American
literary giants, from Washington Irving to Stephen Crane, and assesses their work and its significance for American life and culture.
   ISBN 0-8160-2486-3
     1. American literature—19th century—History and criticism—Juvenile literature.
   2. American literature—Bio—bibliography—Juvenile literature. 3. Authors, American—19th century—Biography—Juvenile literature. [1. American literature—19th century—History and criticism. 2. Authors, American.]   I. Title.   II. Title: 19th century writers.
   III. Series: American profiles series.
PS201.08—dc20   90-20107

A British CIP catalogue record for this book is available from the British Library.

Text design by Ron Monteleone
Jacket design by Ron Monteleone
Composition by Facts On File, Inc.
Manufactured by The Maple-Vail Book Manufacturing Group
Printed in the United States of America

10 9 8 7 6 5 4 3 2 1

This book is printed on acid-free paper.

Contents

46040

Introduction

The 19th century was a time of tremendous growth and change in the United States. In the year 1800, our government was little more than a decade old; there were only 16 states and the rest of the country was mostly an unexplored wilderness. The entire population of the republic was just over five million. Most of these Americans lived by farming. By the end of the century the nation's population had multiplied 15 times, the frontier had disappeared, and the United States had become a modern industrial nation and a world power.

During this period of tremendous growth there were problems and setbacks. Slavery, introduced over 150 years earlier, divided the North and South and finally led to a civil war that threatened the very foundations of our nation. The development of our natural resources and industrialism not only led to great wealth but also to great poverty and injustice. The Native Americans who once inhabited the continent were systematically destroyed or confined to dismal reservations.

As the nation grew, it developed a culture all its own, distinctly different from that of Europe, where the white settlers originally had come from. This American culture was perhaps best represented by its literature. While there were American writers before 1800, it was only when the country was beginning to be settled and civilized that most Americans had the leisure time to pick up a newspaper, read a magazine or ponder over a book.

The intellectual center of the young nation was in the Northeast, particularly New England, which was the first region of the country to be settled. Here education and learning had a long tradition. It is no surprise that nine out of ten of the writers considered in this book were born and raised in New York, New Jersey and Massachusetts. The tenth, Mark Twain, spent most of his productive years as a writer in Connecticut.

These writers were not only geographically linked, but were joined together by a common theme. The pioneer spirit that had

Introduction

built America and the democratic ideals of independence, self-reliance and equality were reflected in their writing. The importance of the individual was integral to their books and characters, whether it be Leatherstocking in his woods, Huck Finn on his river or Thoreau in his cabin on Walden Pond.

As American individualists, these writers were not afraid to criticize and question their country as well as celebrate it. In this sense, like most artists, they were outsiders, looking in at American life and society from their own unique perspective. James Fenimore Cooper, Henry David Thoreau and Walt Whitman, in their essays and poems, challenged our American ideals and values, not to tear them down but to strengthen them. Nathaniel Hawthorne, Herman Melville and Mark Twain explored the dark shadows in our nation's past—exposing Puritan guilt and sin, the bitter fruits of slavery and the delicate balance between good and evil in our society. Stephen Crane dragged American literature into the 20th century with his unique brand of realism that looked unflinchingly at the miseries of city slums and the horrors—as well as the heroism—of modern warfare.

As their ancestors had broken with the colonial past of Great Britain, so these fearless writers often broke with European literary traditions and outmoded forms. They opened new ground in fiction and poetry, and two of them helped to invent an entirely new literary form—the modern short story.

Although today these authors are recognized universally as being great, in their own time their greatness often went unrecognized. Only half of them could be considered successful, and of those, three were plagued by debts and a lack of money despite their fame. Of the rest, one died poor, another forgotten and a third completely unknown to the reading public. All but three of these writers paid to have their first books published, and every one of these works was a dismal failure. It is not surprising that half of these authors didn't want their real names to appear on the title page.

Because of the difficulties of making a living as serious writers, many of them turned to other occupations to support themselves. One was a jack-of-all-trades; three held diplomatic positions abroad; three worked as minor bureaucrats for the government; and four spent a good part of their careers writing and editing newspapers and magazines.

What is truly amazing is that, despite adversity, personal difficulties, an indifferent public and hostile critics, these writers managed to produce so many masterpieces—classic books, stories and poems—that continue to be read and enjoyed today.

This brings us to the purpose of this book. Each brief biography you will read is meant to serve as an introduction to the writers' lives, the times they lived in and, most importantly, their work. A bibliography following each biography gives editions of the writer's work that will be of particular interest to young-adult readers, as well as other biographies and critical studies aimed at this same audience.

It is hoped that, after reading this book, the reader will be encouraged to read the writers' original words. Although these nine men and one woman lived in another century, their writing remains accessible, pertinent and surprisingly entertaining today. Some of these authors are easier to read than others—Hawthorne more so than Melville, Crane more than Cooper, and Dickinson more than Whitman. But with a little effort, there are great pleasures to be gotten from them all.

In the final analysis, literature is not meant to be merely studied, examined and dissected. It is, first and foremost, meant to be read and enjoyed. While the American landscape has changed greatly since the day of these writers, the inner workings of the human heart and mind have not. They speak to us as clearly and profoundly as they did to their contemporaries, if we will only take the time to read and listen.

Washington Irving: America's First Storyteller

America's first truly professional writer, Washington Irving helped create a native literature that won respect in Europe. This portrait hangs in the National Portrait Gallery in Washington, D.C.
(National Portrait Gallery)

*I*magine you are riding horseback down a lonely country road. The hour is midnight. Suddenly up ahead you see a huge figure on a black steed. It is the ghost who haunts this dreaded place—the Headless Horseman! This is the predicament poor Ichabod Crane finds himself in at the climax of perhaps the most famous ghost story in American literature—"The Legend of Sleepy Hollow." While the story is fictitious, its setting is very real. Sleepy Hollow does exist, and in its old graveyard lies a Hessian soldier whose head was knocked off by a cannonball in the Revolutionary War. And not far from his grave lies the man who made the Headless Horseman famous—Washington Irving.

1

Washington Irving was America's first storyteller and man of letters. While there were many Americans who wrote well before Irving, few were known primarily as writers, and none made their living solely from writing. More importantly, Irving's books were read and enjoyed, not just in America, but in Europe as well. With Irving, American literature came of age.

Irving was born in New York City on April 3, 1783. He was the youngest of 11 children. His distant ancestor was the armor-bearer of the great Scottish king Robert the Bruce. Irving's father was a merchant who settled in New York before the Revolution. William Irving was a deacon in the Presbyterian Church and a loving, but stern, father. His wife was gentle and warm—characteristics she passed on to her youngest child.

New York at the time of Irving's birth was a far cry from the teeming metropolis it is today. Then, it was a tiny city of 23,000 people, most of whom lived at the very tip of Manhattan island. Where skyscrapers and busy boulevards stand today were cornfields and pastures full of grazing cows. The Revolutionary War, which had just ended, left New York City in ruins, with half its buildings burned to the ground. For all that, New York had a vitality that already made it a great American city. Ships from all over the world came to its docks to trade. It had a daily newspaper and a theater on Johns Street. It was also the young nation's first capital.

Washington Irving was named for the great American general and the hero of the Revolution—George Washington. In 1789, at New York's Federal Hall, young Irving and his family watched his namesake be inaugurated as the first president of the United States. A short time later, the Irvings' Scottish maid, Lizzie, was walking with young Washington when she spotted the president entering a shop. According to popular legend, the forthright Lizzie walked in and said, "Please, your honor, here's a bairn [Scottish for child] was named after you." The great man put his hand on the six-year-old boy's head and gave him his blessing. Thus, the Father of Our Country met the Father of American Literature.

Irving grew up as a dreamy, idle boy who would rather spend his time reading *Robinson Crusoe* than doing his schoolwork. Exotic adventures and faraway places left him spellbound. At 15, he left school to work in a law office, but the law held little attraction for him; writing, however, did. His older brother Peter was editor of the *Morning Chronicle*, and Irving, then 19, contributed letters to the newspaper. These letters, which poked fun at New York society, were not signed in Irving's name. He used a pen name, or pseudonym—Jonathan Oldstyle, Gentleman. This was a common practice at the time. Humorous or light writing was thought to be too frivolous for a person from a good family to sign his name to. Young Ben Franklin, for example, when writing articles in *his* brother's newspaper, had also used a pseudonym. When older, Franklin attributed many of the proverbs in his famous almanac to a fictional character named Poor Richard.

The New York society Irving wrote about was not an English one, although New York had been an English colony. Before the English, the Dutch had settled the region, calling it New Netherlands, and the little town they established on Manhattan Island, New Amsterdam. Although New Amsterdam was taken over by the British in 1664 and renamed New York, the Dutch people and their culture continued to be dominant in the city and in the villages and towns of the Hudson River Valley to the north.

The Dutch settlers were a superstitious people who loved to tell stories. Every village had its legends and folktales of ghosts and the devil. Even today, their place names conjure up a legendary past—Hell-gate, Storm King, Pirate's Spook and Spuyten Duyvil, which in English means "in spite of the Devil." These legends and stories cast a spell over the impressionable young Irving.

While he had a healthy imagination, Irving had a weak constitution. He developed a nagging cough in his teens that worried his family. To improve his delicate health, his older brothers sent him on a two-year tour of Europe. Irving fell in love with Europe, which had a far richer past than his native country.

On his return to America, Irving began to practice law, but his heart wasn't in it. He turned again to writing and, with his brother William and two friends, wrote and published a satirical magazine called *Salmagundi*. The word means "a mixture of different things" and the magazine was a delightful mix of prose and poetry, most of it humorous and all of it about their hometown, New York City. The first issue came out in January 1807, and was an instant success. Eight hundred copies were sold in just one day.

After a year the magazine folded, the young men having grown weary of it. But from *Salmagundi* Irving got a wonderful idea. Instead of writing magazine pieces, he would write an entire history of New York City, combining fact with fancy. Again, he would use a pseudonym, creating the character of an eccentric old Dutchman and local historian, Diedrich Knickerbocker. The book, published in 1809, bore the unwieldy title *A History of New York from the Beginning of the World to the End of the Dutch Dynasty*. But it became popularly known as *Knickerbocker's History of New York*. Irving's clever mixture of history, humor and folklore was fresh and appealing.

Irving took real historical people from New York's past and transformed them into fabulous figures of folkloric proportion by the use of understatement and exaggeration. Here, for example, is Irving's comic description of Dutch explorer Henry Hudson sighting Manhattan Island for the first time:

> *When the great navigator was first blessed with a view of this enchanting island, he was observed, for the first and only time in his life, to exhibit strong symptoms of astonishment and admiration. He is said to have turned to Master Juet, and uttered these remarkable words, while he pointed towards this paradise of the new world,— "See! there!"—and thereupon, as was always his way when he was uncommonly pleased, he did puff out such clouds of dense tobacco-smoke, that in one minute the vessel was out of sight of land, and Master Juet was fain to wait until the winds dispersed this impenetrable fog.*

New Yorkers chuckled over every page of *Knickerbocker's History*. Some members of old Dutch families took offense at Irving's irreverence, but their protests only made the book more popular than ever. At 26, Washington Irving, who fooled no one with his pseudonym, was the toast of the town. As for Diedrich Knickerbocker, he became forever associated with New York City. To this day, his name lives on in everything from a brand of beer to a professional basketball team.

Although Irving was famous, he still couldn't make a living from his writing. In 1810, he went to work in the family business, a hardware company. These were not happy years for the young author. Matilda Hoffman, a pretty girl he deeply loved, died suddenly at 17. Irving was broken-hearted. Although he would enjoy the company of women all his life, he would never marry. In 1815, he went to England in order to run a branch of the company. It was to have been a short stay. As it turned out, Irving remained in Europe for 17 years.

He arrived in England to find himself a literary sensation. A friend had passed out copies of *Knickerbocker's History*, and several well-known writers had read and loved it. These included the Romantic poets Samuel Taylor Coleridge and George, Lord

Byron, and novelist Sir Walter Scott. Irving visited Scott at his medieval home, Abbotsford, and found they shared a deep love of the romantic past.

Europe and its rich heritage inspired Irving to write his second and best book, *The Sketch Book of Geoffery Crayon, Gentleman*. It contained not only short sketches, or impressions, of places Irving had visited, but essays and short stories. Two of these stories are the works on which Irving's reputation rests today—"Rip Van Winkle" and "The Legend of Sleepy Hollow." Ironically, these two most American of stories were based on German folktales. But by transplanting the tales to the Hudson River Valley and adding American characters to the European plots, Irving created a native literature as charming as it is sometimes grotesque.

"The Legend of Sleepy Hollow" isn't so much about ghosts as it is about the grip superstition held on the imaginations of his characters. It is often forgotten that the Headless Horseman was actually Brom Bones, schoolmaster Ichabod Crane's rival for the hand of a pretty farmer's daughter. Brom masquerades as the legendary ghost to frighten off poor Ichabod and succeeds in the story's riveting climax. Irving, always the sly storyteller, never states this outright, but lets the reader come to his own conclusion.

The supernatural in "Rip Van Winkle" is very real, but Rip's encounter with the ghosts of Henry Hudson and his crew is ultimately a happy one. After drinking Hudson's heady brew, Rip sleeps for 20 years. He awakens to find himself a stranger in his own village. In this excerpt, poor, confused Rip meets his daughter and grandson:

> . . . *a fresh, comely woman pressed through the throng to get a peep at the gray-breaded man. She had a chubby child in her arms, which, frightened at his looks, began to cry. "Hush, Rip," cried she, "hush, you little fool; the old man won't hurt you." The name of the child, the air of the mother, the tone of her voice, all awakened a train of recollections in his mind.*
>
> *"What is your name, my good woman?" asked he.*
>
> *"Judith Gardenier."*
>
> *"And your father's name?"*
>
> *"Ah, poor man, Rip Van Winkle was his name, but it's twenty years since he went away from home . . . but whether he shot himself, or was carried away by the Indians, nobody can tell, I was then but a little girl."*
>
> *Rip had but one more question to ask; but he put it with a faltering voice:*

5

*"Rip Van Winkle" is one of Irving's
most popular stories. It has been a
favorite with illustrators and artists
since it first appeared in 1820. This
picture of Rip fishing accompanied
an early edition of the story.*
(Library of Congress)

"Where's your mother?"
*Oh, she, too, had died but a short time since; she broke a blood-
vessel in a fit of passion at a New England peddler.*
*There was a drop of comfort, at least, in this intelligence. The honest
man could contain himself no longer. He caught his daughter and
her child in his arms. "I am your father!" cried he—"Young Rip Van
Winkle once—old Rip Van Winkle now—Does nobody know poor Rip
Van Winkle!"*

The story ends with Rip living to a ripe old age, surrounded by
his children and grandchildren. In both these stories, Irving captures the lazy, happy and comical life of the Dutch villages of New
York. Both Rip and Ichabod are such memorable characters that
they have entered our folklore alongside such larger-than-life
figures as Johnny Appleseed, Paul Bunyan and Pecos Bill.

Readers in America and England were entranced by Irving's ingenious tales. Thanks to him, America was no longer looked down on by Europeans as a cultural wasteland. It now had a literary tradition of its own, one that would grow fruitfully in the next few generations. Ironically, Irving, as a writer, would not grow with it.

His next book, *Bracebridge Hall*, grew out of a Christmas holiday Irving spent at an English country manor. While its style was similar to *The Sketch Book*, it was not popular with the reading public. Irving continued to travel throughout Europe, soaking up culture and history wherever he went.

In 1826, he visited Spain, where he would serve as a junior diplomat for the United States government. Irving's easygoing and sociable manner made him ideally suited to be a diplomat. However, he found the give and take of politics distasteful. Spain itself he found fascinating, and he fell in love with the countryside and its people. The strange mixture of European and Islamic traditions mesmerized him.

No place attracted him more than the Moorish palace in the city of Grenada known as the Alhambra. The Moors were Arabs from North Africa who conquered Spain in the 700s. They built the Alhambra in the 13th century as a home for their kings and a fortress to defend their shrinking Spanish kingdom. With its vast red wall, 13 towers and exquisitely designed inner courts, the Alhambra was, and still is, a magical place. In Irving's day, the halls of the palace were filled with old women and hang-abouts who sat for hours gossiping and telling stories. Irving listened to these stories day after day and adopted many of them into his next book, *Legends of the Alhambra*. It quickly became one of his most popular works.

However, the vitality and originality of his writing was fading. There was a robust humor and vigorous energy in his first two books that was missing from his later works. The more Irving immersed himself in exotic places and European traditions, the more removed he became from the source of his inspiration—his native land. His writing, while still polished and often charming, was becoming increasingly more stylized and derivative.

In 1829, Irving returned to England, where he became part of the United States diplomatic staff in London. He sailed home three years later. He was 50 and a famous author with an international reputation. America welcomed him with open arms.

Like his character Rip Van Winkle, who awoke after a 20-year sleep to find his hometown a strange and startling place, Irving found America a far different country from the one he had left. There were 19 states when he departed; now there were 24. New York had grown into a thriving, prosperous city. The young and the adventurous were looking westward for new land and fresh opportunities.

To get a better grasp on these changes in the country, Irving decided to see the West for himself. His route took him along the Ohio and Mississippi rivers. He met Indians, marveled at vast herds of buffalo and ate deer meat, better known as venison. Not a writer to waste any new experience, he put down his adventures in a book, *A Tour of the Prairies*, published in 1835.

All the years of restless travel had taken their toll. Irving, at last, was ready to settle down. The area he chose was his beloved Hudson River Valley: the spot, the sleepy village of Tarrytown, the setting of "The Legend of Sleepy Hollow." Tarrytown was named, as Irving himself pointed out in his story, for the local Dutch farmers who liked to "tarry" at the inns on market day.

Sunnyside in Irvington, New York, was Irving's home for the last 25 years of his life. It was originally an old Dutch cottage that he renovated to reflect his own colorful personality. Today it is open to the public for guided tours.
(Library of Congress)

The home Irving chose for himself was a small, stone Dutch cottage that overlooked the Hudson, not far from the Sleepy Hollow churchyard. With the help of an architect friend, Irving enlarged the cottage and put his own cosmopolitan stamp on it. The exterior design was a charming mixture of Dutch, English, Spanish and even Chinese architecture. In a letter to a brother he called his new home "a quaint, picturesque little pile." A congenial gathering place for Irving's family, friends and fellow writers, the home lived up to its name—Sunnyside. Today Sunnyside is a museum, lovingly cared for and kept much the way it looked in Irving's day. The village it lies in, once a part of Tarrytown, was renamed Irvington after the author's death.

Irving was content to live out his days at Sunnyside. But in 1842 duty beckoned. President John Tyler appointed him U.S. minister to Spain. Irving didn't want to accept, but he knew there was no one better equipped for the position. He knew the language and the culture of Spain intimately, and was highly respected by the Spanish.

He returned home four years later, weary of international diplomacy and ready to return to writing. He went to work on his last and most ambitious literary work. Irving had always felt a strong bond with the man whose name he bore. Years earlier, he had been urged by a close friend to write a biography of Washington. He had written several other biographies—of Christopher Columbus, English author Oliver Goldsmith and Mahomet, founder of Islam. But Irving's *Life of George Washington* would surpass them all in length and detail. When finished, the work was five volumes long—the first complete biography of our first president, and the only one for many years.

Irving died shortly after completing the last volume, on a beautiful autumn day in 1859. It was the same kind of day on which Rip Van Winkle set off on his fateful hunting trip. Washington Irving was 76 years old when he died, and the grand old man of American letters.

While other American authors' reputations have grown steadily with the passing of years, Irving's has shrunk. His biographies and histories, while gracefully written, have been surpassed by more recent writers with a better historical perspective. His travel stories and exotic tales are largely forgotten. Even *Knickerbocker's History*, one of his finest books, is little read today.

Irving found his literary voice at an early age, only to lose it by imitating older voices of European literature. As Charles Dudley

Warner, one of Irving's first biographers, points out, "His face was set towards the past, not towards the future. He never caught the restlessness of this [the 19th] century." It might be noted that while Irving's past was quaint, colorful and picturesque, the past explored by his young contemporaries Edgar Allan Poe, Nathaniel Hawthorne and later, Herman Melville, was far more compelling and profound.

But without Irving, these other writers might not have risen to such heights. He made America and its literature respectable in the hallowed halls of Europe. This was undoubtedly his greatest act of diplomacy. He also established the short story as an important form in American literature, paving the way for Poe and Hawthorne, who would become masters of the form. Poe would later pay Irving the ultimate compliment by calling him "the most deservedly eminent among all the pioneers of American literature." Irving's use of American settings and characters influenced James Fenimore Cooper and many other writers. His humorous storytelling style had an important impact on Mark Twain, Bret Harte and O. Henry.

Perhaps the American author whose career most closely parallels Irving's is Twain. He too loved to travel, and became a celebrated man of letters. However, Twain turned bitter in his old age, both from private tragedies and the changes he saw in the world around him. Irving suffered no such anguish. The America he left when he died was changing but had not yet suffered a bloody civil war and a major industrial revolution.

Of all the writers we will be considering, Washington Irving's talent was the most modest, but in many ways, he lived the happiest life. The great 19th-century authors to come after him were in their own ways, driven by demons, devils and the dark side of the American dream.

Chronology

April 3, 1783 born in New York City

1802 first humorous writings appear in brother Peter's newspaper, the *Morning Chronicle*

1807–08 publishes satirical magazine *Salmagundi* with brother William and friends

1809 first book, *Knickerbocker's History of New York*, published

1815 travels to England, beginning a 17-year stay in Europe

1820 *The Sketch Book* appears, including "Rip Van Winkle" and "The Legend of Sleepy Hollow"

1826 receives diplomatic post in Spain

1832 *Legends of the Alhambra*, a collection of exotic tales, published; same year returns to the United States

1835 settles in Tarrytown, New York at Sunnyside

1842 appointed U.S. minister to Spain

1846 returns home and begins his last work, *The Life of George Washington*

November 28, 1859 dies at Sunnyside

Further Reading

Irving's Works

Knickerbocker's History of New York, edited by Anne Carroll Moore (Garden City, N.Y.: Doubleday, 1928). A very readable edition of Irving's first book, beautifully illustrated by James Daugherty.

Rip Van Winkle and Other Stories (Garden City, N.Y.: Doubleday, 1955). This volume, aimed at young adults, includes the two best-known tales and other lesser-known but interesting stories.

Books About Washington Irving

Van Wyck Brooks, *The World of Washington Irving* (New York: E.P. Dutton, 1944). A comprehensive study of the American literary scene in the first part of the 19th century; also includes essays on James Fenimore Cooper and Edgar Allan Poe.

Catherine Owens Peace, *Washington Irving: His Life* (New York: Holt, 1957). A semi-fictionalized but informative biography, stressing Irving's early years.

Anya Seton, *Washington Irving* (Boston: Houghton Mifflin, 1960). A more full-bodied biography than the Peace book, with well-selected quotes from the author's work and excellent illustrations by Harve Stein.

James Fenimore Cooper: Myth Maker of the West

This engraving shows James Fenimore Cooper, the successful author, at home. Cooper wrote 50 books, including novels of all types, essays and histories. He was the most prolific of the great 19th-century American writers.
(Library of Congress)

*T*he scene is a country house in upstate New York. The year, 1819. It is evening and the gentleman of the house is reading aloud to his wife in front of a roaring fire. The book is the latest romantic novel from England by a lady author. The reader, a man with little patience for foolishness, suddenly tosses the novel aside after only a few pages. "I could write you a better book than that myself!" he proclaims to his surprised spouse. The idea amuses her. She challenges her impetuous husband, who has written nothing more taxing than a letter, to write a better book. Before the night is out, he has written an entire chapter of a novel. Thus at the age of 30, the career of James Fenimore Cooper, America's first great novelist, is launched.

It was not an auspicious beginning. Cooper's first novel, *Precaution*, published in 1820 at the author's own expense, was an artistic and commercial failure. But he enjoyed writing it and decided to try again. This time, he looked for a subject that would truly interest an American audience—and himself.

One of Cooper's neighbors in Westchester County was founding father and former chief justice of the United States John Jay. Jay was a good storyteller and enjoyed entertaining his friends with true tales about the American Revolution, fought over 40 years earlier. One story that particularly impressed Cooper was about a secret agent Jay had employed to gather news of British strategy behind enemy lines. This spy was no daring hero, but a simple peddler who had outsmarted the British with his shrewd Yankee ingenuity.

The novel, *The Spy*, published in 1821, was an immediate success. For the first time, Americans could read a novel about an American hero that glorified their own recent past. The book was so entertaining that even the British, many of whom still resented losing their American colonies, read it eagerly. The gentleman farmer was now a successful gentleman author. Over the next 30 years, Cooper would write nearly 50 more books, 29 of them novels.

James Fenimore Cooper was born into a world of wealth and privilege on September 14, 1789. His father, William Cooper, was a respected judge and one of the richest landowners in New York State. Born in Burlington, New Jersey, Cooper grew up in Cooperstown, founded and named after his father. At the time, Cooperstown, 150 miles north of New York City, was still a frontier town, surrounded by deep forests and clear, blue lakes. Most of the Indians were gone, but the stories young Cooper heard from the older pioneers stirred his imagination, much as the Dutch legends of the Hudson Valley excited the young Washington Irving.

Cooper entered Yale at age 13, the youngest member of his class. Although he was a good student, his love of pranks surpassed his love of learning. When he set off a charge of gunpowder in the door lock of an unpopular teacher, Cooper was expelled. He returned to Cooperstown, but found country life at the family homestead too tame for his high spirits. A year later, at 17, he signed on with the new United States Navy as a common sailor and boarded a ship sailing for England. He loved the sea as much as he had loved the wilderness. In less than two years Cooper was promoted to midshipman.

Tragedy struck the Coopers in 1809. Judge Cooper, an outspoken man with many enemies, was shot on the steps of the state capitol in Albany by a political opponent. He died three weeks later. Young Cooper inherited his father's sizable estate. In 1811, he married the pretty Susan De Lancey, resigned from the Navy and returned home to Cooperstown. He became a gentleman farmer, dabbling profitably in wool and whale-oil. He might have lived out his days as a contented man of leisure if not for that poor, nameless novel his wife had brought home one day.

With the success of *The Spy*, Cooper and his family moved to New York City, where they lived in lavish style. A large, robust man with piercing gray eyes, Cooper soon had a reputation as "the handsomest man in New York." Eager to begin a new novel, he turned this time to his beloved Cooperstown for a setting. He changed its name to Templeton and set his story in 1793. He called the novel *The Pioneers*. Its central character was not a member of the community, but an outsider, an old scout and woodsman with the unlikely name of Natty Bumppo.

Natty was a frontiersman, living in the wilderness among the Indians, whom he both fought and befriended. He was as fine a shot with his rifle Killdeer as Davy Crockett (without the boasting) and as great a trailblazer as Daniel Boone. He was modest, manly, a master of every kind of woodlore. His story, which Cooper would continue to tell in four more novels, was the story of America. *The Pioneers* ends with Natty heading further West, away from encroaching civilization, to find new frontiers.

Leatherstocking Tales, as the five novels came to be called, traced Natty's life in the wilderness. Written out of sequence, the last book, *The Deerslayer* (1841), is actually the first chronologically, presenting Natty as a young scout. In *The Last of the Mohicans* (1826), he is an experienced woodsman in his thirties. In *The Pathfinder* (1840), Cooper's personal favorite, Natty is middle-aged, and in *The Prairie* (1827), he dies an old man among the Pawnee Indians on the Great Plains. Natty appears under different names in the saga—Hawkeye, Leatherstocking, the Long Rifle—but his courage, skill, honor and deep understanding of life's mysteries remain consistent throughout.

In Natty Bumppo, Cooper created the first true American folk hero, and in the *Leatherstocking Tales*, the first "Westerns." These exciting tales of pursuit, escape and daring rescues in the wilderness became the archetype for thousands of novels and, later, movies. The Western myth and the Western hero—strong, silent, solitary—begin with Cooper. Natty's long shadow reaches down to John Wayne and even Rambo.

However, Cooper's powers of description and his skillful storytelling place him far above his many imitators. This is not to say he is without his flaws. Cooper was as impetuous in his writing as he was in everything else. He wrote quickly and prolifically, and, as one critic has noted, even his best books "are marked by both grandeur of conception and carelessness of detail." A glaring example of his carelessness occurs in one novel where he renames his heroine halfway through the story! Logic is often lost in the headlong plunge of his narratives. In *The Last of the Mohicans*, his most commonly read book today, the daughters of a British commander in the French and Indian Wars are tossed in and out of danger with the regularity of an old-time movie serial but with little logic.

As for Cooper's literary style, it was considered old-fashioned and stuffy even in his own day. Natty often breaks into long-winded, philosophical speeches, even at the most inappropriate times. On the verge of an attack, another character tells him, "This is a subject that might better be discussed another time." The effect on a modern-day reader is unintentionally hilarious. Mark Twain, who owed much more to Cooper than he probably cared to admit, wrote a wicked attack on him in "Fenimore Cooper's Literary Offenses." According to Twain, the old master broke "eighteen" of the "nineteen rules governing literary art."

But taking all his offenses into account does not diminish Cooper's power to tell a story. When the time comes for action, the setting, characters and plot spring to life with a vividness and clarity few modern writers can match. Here, for example, is an excerpt from the climactic moments of *The Last of the Mohicans*. Uncas, the title character and son of Natty's Indian companion, Chingachgook, has just died on a rocky ledge at the hands of the evil Huron Magua. Magua makes his escape as Natty rushes to the scene:

Then Magua issued from a crevice, and stepping with calm indiffer-
ence over the body of the last of his associates, he leaped a wide fissure,
and ascended the rocks . . .A single bound would carry him to the
brow of the precipice, and assure his safety. Before taking the leap,
however, the Huron paused, and shaking his hand at the scout, he
shouted—
"The palefaces are dogs! the Delawares women! Magua leaves them
on the rocks, for the crows!"
Laughing hoarsely, he made a desperate leap, and fell short of his
mark; though his hands grasped a shrub on the verge of the height.
The form of Hawkeye had crouched like a beast about to take its
spring, and his frame trembled so violently with eagerness, that the
muzzle of the half-raised rifle played like a leaf fluttering in the wind.
Without exhausting himself with fruitless efforts, the cunning Magua
suffered his body to drop to the length of his arms, and found a
fragment for his feet to rest on. Then summoning all his powers, he
renewed the attempt, and so far succeeded, as to draw his knees on
the edge of the mountain. It was now, when the body of his enemy
was most collected together, that the agitated weapon of the scout was
drawn to his shoulder. The surrounding rocks, themselves, were not
steadier than the piece became, for the single instant that it poured
out its contents. The arms of the Huron relaxed, and his body fell back
a little, while his knees still kept their position. Turning a relentless
look on his enemy, he shook a hand in grim defiance. But his hold
loosened, and his dark person was seen cutting the air with its head
downward, for a fleeting instant, until it glided past the fringe of
shrubbery which clung to the mountain, in its rapid flight to destruc-
tion.

Such marvelous action sequences are heightened by Cooper's exquisite word paintings of the landscapes against which his characters fight to the death, whether it be the forests surrounding the pioneer village of Cooperstown or the vast watery reaches of Lake George.

Finally there is the scope of Cooper's imagination, which en- compasses not just the lifetime of his mythical hero but that of the American wilderness itself, from colonial days to the growing years of the young republic. As historian Allan Nevins has percep- tively written, "Those who take the pains to read the five novels attentively, taking them in proper succession from Deerslayer's awkward youth to the trapper's mellow old age, will find that they have read nothing less than the nearest approach yet made to an American epic."

There is another side to Cooper the writer that few readers today are aware of. Besides creating the Western, he also wrote the first true sea tale. In 1823, after reading a novel by English author Sir Walter Scott, Cooper complained that the book was filled with so many inaccuracies about life at sea that it would make a sailor laugh. As with his first novel, Cooper took up the challenge to write his own sea novel. The result was *The Pilot*, the first American novel that dealt with the sailor's life. The book introduced Long Tom Coffin, a water-bound version of Natty Bumppo, and became a best-seller. Cooper wrote a dozen more tales of the sea, some of them among his best works.

In 1826, after the international success of *The Last of the Mohicans*, Cooper sailed for Europe with his wife, four daughters and son. Like Irving before him, he would fall under the spell of Europe and its rich, centuries-old culture. For seven years the Coopers traveled around the continent, marveling at everything they saw. The tireless author continued to write steadily. When friends expressed amazement at how he could turn out so many books while sightseeing, his reply in a letter was, "I wear an inkhorn at my buttonhole." His American novels written abroad rank among his best, but when he turned to Europe for a setting in two books, the results were disappointing. It was time to head for home.

As it had been for Irving, America was a different place for the returning Cooper. New York City was crowded and dirty. People seemed more concerned with making money than enjoying life, and everyone was in a hurry. Andrew Jackson was president, ushering in a new era of democracy where the common American was exalted to new heights. Cooper was a staunch supporter of democracy but he found Jacksonian America disturbing. He felt many of his countrymen were crude and unmannerly, and the country in danger of becoming a "mobocracy."

In 1834 he wrote a book of essays he called *A Letter To His Countrymen*. Many readers saw the author's praise of Europe and its traditions in this book as an implicit criticism of America. Cooper, the celebrator of the American frontier and pioneer spirit, had turned into one of the country's severest critics. The public didn't like that one bit.

Sales of Cooper's books began to drop. Worse still, he was bitterly attacked, often unfairly, by newspapers across the coun-

This illustration from The Deerslayer *shows its hero, Natty Bumppo, with the heroine, Judith Hutter. Their romance did not work out, and Natty returns to the woods, a confirmed bachelor. This serialized version of the novel appeared long after its first publication. However, it was not unusual in the 19th century for an author's work to appear in newspapers or magazines before appearing in book form.*
(Library of Congress)

try. When New York's *Commercial Advertiser* ran a stinging review of his latest book, a *History of the United States Navy*, Cooper filed a lawsuit against the paper's editor, William Stone. The review claimed the book was filled with inaccuracies and called the author unpatriotic. The case dragged on in the courts for three long years. Finally Cooper won, after delivering an eloquent eight-hour defense of his history. Although this lawsuit, and many others, drained the writer's energy and finances, they helped to establish better and stricter libel laws. In the future, anyone who injured another person's reputation unjustly in print would be committing a crime and would be punishable under the law.

Cooper's problems didn't end here, however. As he grew older, he grew more stubborn and cantankerous, much like his father before him. Cooper couldn't even get along with his neighbors in Cooperstown, where he had restored his ancestral home, Otsego Hall, and "retired." Amid these public troubles, the aging author retreated further into the past he loved, tracing the forest trails with the young Natty Bumppo in *The Deerslayer* and *The Pathfinder*. The public's response to these fine novels, ironically, was tepid. As the nation progressed into the industrial age, interest in the past was fading.

Like the older Natty, who was misunderstood by the new settlers disrupting his simple Eden, Cooper found himself more and more isolated by the modern, materialistic society that now surrounded him. He wrote a trilogy of novels, *The Littlepage Manuscripts*, that fervently defended the landed gentry as an enlightened force in unruly American society. He firmly believed it was people such as himself who alone could save democracy from its excesses. Yet, even as he condemned the new society, Cooper himself was caught up in it. Many of the books he wrote in his last decade were written quickly and carelessly to make a fast buck, and were far inferior to his best work.

James Fenimore Cooper died in Cooperstown on September 14, 1851, one day before his 62nd birthday. His beloved wife Susan survived him by only four months. Otsego Hall was soon sold to strangers and was destroyed shortly after in a fire.

For all his faults as a writer, Cooper's place in American literature is a secure one. If Washington Irving created our national literature, Cooper gave it a firm foundation. Irving remained basically a regionalist in his writing, while Cooper, as critic Van Wyck Brooks points out, had an "all-American imagination" that encompassed the nation. He chartered his country's story on land and sea, and in every kind of fiction from adventure tales to historical novels, romances and even satires. His sea stories prefigured Herman Melville's exotic South Sea adventures and the whaling epic *Moby-Dick*. His perceptive social criticism paved the way for the thoughtful essays of Henry David Thoreau and the biting satires of Mark Twain, who lived in a later, much greedier America.

Cooper's great protagonist, Natty Bumppo, brought a new kind of hero onto the literary landscape, and *Leatherstocking Tales* created a genre of fiction, the Western, that is still with us today. The myth itself of the American West, as a place where people can find renewal in nature and live free and equal, grew largely out of Cooper's saga. He was also the first American author to look seriously, if not always sympathetcially, at the American Indian. While celebrating the Indian's way of life and culture, he also saw that, like whites, they had a capacity for both good and evil.

As he grew older, Cooper lost touch with America, focusing on small problems while overlooking the larger significance of our growing democracy. However, he criticized America out of a deep love and concern for his native land—a tradition that would be carried forward by Thoreau, Ralph Waldo Emerson and a host of lesser writers and thinkers in the second half of the 19th century. Cooper established the American writer as both a popular spokesperson for his country and, at the same time, a suspicious outsider—a misunderstood, alienated figure in a rapidly changing society. This was a role that the great writers who would follow him would continue to play.

Chronology

━━━━━━━━━━

September 15, 1789   born in Burlington, New Jersey

1802   enters Yale University, youngest in his class

1806–11   serves in United States Navy

1811   marries Susan De Lancey and becomes a gentleman farmer

1820   writes first novel, *Precaution*, on a bet with his wife

1821   *The Spy* appears, first important American novel

1823   *The Pilot*, first American sea novel, and *The Pioneers*, first of the *Leatherstocking Tales*, published

1826–1833   lives abroad in Europe

1826   *The Last of the Mohicans* published, his most popular work

1833   returns to United States and settles in Cooperstown, New York

1834   *A Letter to His Countrymen*, first work critical of America appears

1840   *The Pathfinder* published

1841   *The Deerslayer*, last of the *Leatherstocking Tales*, but first in chronological order, appears

September 14, 1851   dies at Cooperstown

Further Reading

Cooper's Works

The Leatherstocking Saga, edited by Allan Nevins and illustrated by Reginald Marsh. (New York: Pantheon Books, 1954). This indispensable volume contains all five *Leatherstocking Tales* in chronological order and abridged for modern readers. Nevins's introductory essays on Cooper and his work are excellent.

The Pioneers (New York: Holt, 1967). A good edition of the complete novel, the first *Leatherstocking* tale Cooper wrote, with an informative introduction by Leon Howard.

The Spy (New York: Dodd, Mead, 1946). The Great Illustrated Classic edition of Cooper's first successful novel, with a foreword by Curtis Dahl.

Books About James Fenimore Cooper

Isabel Proudfit, *James Fenimore Cooper* (New York: Julian Messner, 1946). A better-than-average young-adult biography of the author, although somewhat dated.

Edgar Allan Poe: Master of the Macabre

The gloomy expression on Edgar Allan Poe's face in this early photograph, called a daguerreotype, probably came from pondering his debts and not his next tale of horror. Poe spent most of his career as a writer and editor one step away from the poorhouse.
(Library of Congress)

*T*here are a few writers who do not easily fit into categories, historical periods or national literatures. Their work seems to grow not from the world around them but from the inner realities of their lives, passions, fears and obsessions. It is this that makes them unique and remarkable. Such a writer was Edgar Allan Poe. Short-story writer, poet and critic, Poe is a strange and original figure in American literature. There has been no one quite like him before or since.

***

As with other artists whose lives have been full of strife and turmoil, Poe the man has become inseparable from Poe the writer. No American author has been more written about, and yet no American author has been more misunderstood.

Poe was the creator of some of the most frightening tales of horror in world literature, and because of this many people have concluded he must have been something of a monster himself. Writers and biographers have described him variously as a libertine, an alcoholic, a wild bohemian, a madman, a drug addict and a Satanist. In reality, he was none of these. Poe did have a drinking problem in his last years, but it arose out of an extremely low tolerance for alcohol rather than a deep dependence on it. In his personal life, Poe was basically a gentle, thoughtful, industrious, middle-class person who was beset throughout his life with trouble and tragedy. Despite his extraordinary talents, he never enjoyed the fame or wealth of Irving, Cooper, Hawthorne and other lesser contemporaries. For most of his professional career, he stood precariously on the brink of poverty. What is remarkable is that in spite of this, he was able to transform his personal problems and deepest fears into great literature.

Edgar Allan Poe's troubles started almost from the moment he entered the world. He was born in Boston on January 19, 1809, to a pair of struggling actors. The theatrical world, with its sense of melodrama and illusion, would leave its stamp on his life and work. His father, David Poe of Baltimore, deserted the family soon after Poe's birth and was never heard of again. His mother, Elizabeth Arnold Poe, a genteel woman, died at age 24 when he was only three. Poe's two sisters were adopted by friends of the family. Edgar was taken in by John Allan, a wealthy tobacco merchant, and his wife, Frances, of Richmond, Virginia. Allan never legally adopted Poe, but this didn't stop him from trying to dictate the boy's future as he grew older.

From 1815 to 1820, the Allans lived in England, where the young Poe attended a private school. Here he first fell under the spell of the Romantic poets whose works were changing the literary landscape of Europe. Although a lover of poetry, Poe was far from the dreamy, shadowy figure many people have imagined. He was a handsome, somewhat spoiled youth who was a good student, a leader and a sportsman. Since the Allans were childless, he stood to inherit three-quarters of a million dollars on his foster father's death. But as one critic has observed, Poe's seemingly charmed life "was built on quicksand."

In 1826 he entered the University of Virginia, where he was a top scholar and a voracious reader of arcane books and magazines of every kind. Mass-circulation magazines were something new in America at that time. As the young country prospered and people had more leisure time, especially in the cities, there grew a vast new educated public, anxious to read about current events and new developments in the arts and sciences. Magazines by the dozens sprang up to meet this demand, and with them, a new kind of literary man was born—the professional magazine writer and editor. It was the kind of career that would appeal to Poe as he grew older.

John Allan was not pleased with his ward's literary interests. He wanted him to be a lawyer. To show his displeasure, or simply out of spite, Allan sent the student the smallest of allowances. Poe was forced to find other ways to meet his college expenses and turned to gambling. His luck was poor, and he soon had heavy debts. Allan, enraged by this behavior, pulled Poe out of school before he had finished his first year.

The relationship between ward and foster father grew steadily worse. In March 1827, Poe ran away from home and went to Boston, where he enlisted in the Army under the name "Edgar A. Perry." If military life did not agree with Poe, it was not immediately apparent. He rose to the rank of sergeant-major before being honorably discharged in 1829. The same year Frances Allan, whom Poe loved dearly, died. Longing for a family to give stability to his stormy life, he visited his aunt, Maria Clemm, and her young daughter, Virginia, in Baltimore.

However, Poe did not entirely turn away from his foster father, who had remarried. He decided to give the military life another try, and asked Allan to help him get an appointment to the U.S. Military Academy at West Point. Allan did so, and Poe went off to become an officer. But by now his attraction to writing had become very strong. (Poe had already written two volumes of poetry, which he had published privately.) He grew increasingly frustrated with the strict discipline of West Point. He deliberately broke a rule by missing chapel and was asked to leave.

He returned to Baltimore and moved in with his aunt and cousin, the two people in the world he felt closest to. They lived in genteel poverty, mostly from Aunt Clemm's wages as a seamstress. In 1831, Poe published his third book, called simply *Poems*. It contained some very good romantic poems, including "To Helen" and "The City in the Sea." The public, however, took little notice, and in frustration, Poe turned to writing fiction.

Short stories, made popular in America by Washington Irving, appeared regularly in magazines and even newspapers of the day. Poe started writing stories in earnest and sold five of them in 1832. The following year, his story "MS. Found in a Bottle" won first prize in a short-story contest, earning him the princely sum of $50. The young man's literary career was officially launched. More important than the prize money was the friendship Poe formed with novelist John P. Kennedy. Kennedy helped the promising writer get a job as editor of a local magazine, *The Southern Literary Messenger*.

The magazine was in bad shape when Poe took it over. But through hard work and talent, he quickly turned it into a success, increasing subscriptions from 500 to over 3,500. With a secure job and a growing literary reputation, Poe was ready to help his poor relations. He had fallen in love with his cousin two years before but planned to put off marrying her. Now he thought delay would only worsen their circumstances, and on May 16, 1836, the 27-year-old Poe married Virginia Clemm, not yet 14. This may seem shocking to us today, but in 19th-century society, 15 or 16 was the average age of marriage for women.

Supporting three people on his meager salary of $10 a week was nearly impossible, and Poe resigned from his job as editor and moved to New York in 1837 to find a more promising position. As opposed to Irving and Cooper, New York held few charms for Poe. His genteel Southern sensibilities were offended by the brash, fast-paced Northern city. In the year and a half he spent there, however, he wrote and published his only novel, the fantastic *Narrative of Arthur Gordon Pym*. It was the story of a stowaway on a whaling ship who undergoes various adventures, including a mutiny and an attack from cannibals. He ends up floating in a canoe at the South Pole, where he undergoes a transforming experience. Already Poe was showing a keen interest in the strange and the bizarre.

The small family moved to Philadelphia, where Poe found more work as an editor, but his growing literary reputation had little effect on his income. As editor and critic, Poe believed firmly that American literature was ready to be judged by the same high standards as the literature of Europe. His sharp critical eye made him many enemies as well as some lasting friendships. He reviewed, among others, books by Nathaniel Hawthorne and the poet Henry Wadsworth Longfellow.

All the while, Poe was turning out his own highly original stories. In 1840, his short-story collection, *Tales of the Grotesque and Arabesque*, appeared. The 25 tales in this work were like nothing else in American literature. Like Irving, Poe was attracted to ghost stories and the supernatural. But while Irving wrote charming tales told by a detached storyteller, Poe's tales of horror were twisted, tormented descents into the author's own fearful nightmares. It is this personal intensity, more than any other literary characteristic, that make Poe's best tales so haunting and unforgettable.

The same terrible themes occur in story after story. Poe had a morbid fear of being buried alive, and the subject figures in such classic tales as "The Fall of the House of Usher," "The Black Cat," "The Cask of Amontillado" and the partly autobiographical "The Premature Burial." Another favorite theme was revenge and madness, which figured heavily in "Hop-Frog," "The Cask of Amontillado" and "The Tell-Tale Heart."

This last story is told, like most of the tales, in the first person. The narrator is a madman who murders a fellow boarder in a rooming house because he believes he is being bewitched by the poor victim's unclosing eye. He dismembers the corpse and buries the parts under the floorboards in his room. When the police come to question him, the murderer begins to hear the beating of the dead man's heart. The beating grows louder and louder, until the man blurts out his confession to make it cease. The reader is left to believe that it was the murderer's own guilty conscience that led to his ruin. Such piercing psychological insight was new to literature and derived in part from Poe's keen interest in the latest developments in science and technology.

This interest in science led Poe to create an entirely different kind of story. With his character the Frenchman C. Auguste Dupin, he fashioned the world's first amateur detective, and in the three stories Dupin appeared in, he launched the modern mystery story. Mysteries had been written before Poe, but never before had a crime been presented as a puzzle to be solved by a logical mind.

"The Pit and the Pendulum" was one of Poe's most celebrated tales. Despite the terrible ordeal faced by the hero in this graphic illustration, he is actually saved from the pendulum blade by the rats who gnaw through the ropes that bind him.
(Library of Congress)

"The Murders in the Rue Morgue" is perhaps the most famous of his "tales of ratiocination," or reasoning, as Poe called them. In this story, a mother and daughter are horribly murdered in their home, in a room that is apparently locked from the inside. The Paris police are completely baffled about how the murderer made his escape, but the clever Dupin gets to the solution by carefully following clues and using his well-developed powers of deduction. The killer is exposed and found to be a runaway ape, who used his long arms to swing outside the window from one ledge to another.

Mystery writers from Arthur Conan Doyle, the creator of Sherlock Holmes, onward, have expressed their indebtedness to Poe. As Doyle once wrote about the detective story, "On this narrow path the writer must walk, and he sees the footmarks of Poe always in front of him." The highest award in mystery fiction today is called the "Edgar" in Poe's honor.

Interestingly enough, Poe didn't think very highly of his detective stories, or, for that matter, of any of his fiction. He considered himself, first and foremost, a poet. In 1845, a year after returning to New York City, he finally found a wide audience for his poetry when he published his collection *The Raven and Other Poems*. "The Raven" became an instant success and remains one of the best-known poems in the English language. The mood and setting of this gripping ballad is typical Poe:

> *Once upon a midnight dreary, while I pondered, weak and weary,*
> *Over many a quaint and curious volume of forgotten lore—*
> *While I nodded, nearly napping, suddenly there came a tapping,*
> *As of someone gently rapping, rapping at my chamber door.*
> *" 'Tis some visitor," I muttered, "tapping at my chamber door—*
> *Only this and nothing more."*

The long rhythmic lines, the intricate internal rhymes and the effective repetitions give the poem a musical flow and a dramatic intensity that carries the story forward and the reader with it. The "visitor" turns out to be a raven, who startles the narrator from thoughts of his dead love. To every question the tormented man puts to it, the black bird replies, "Nevermore!" He becomes convinced the raven is an evil spirit come to haunt him.

> *"Be that word our sign of parting, bird or fiend!" I shrieked, upstarting—*
> *"Get thee back into the tempest and the night's Plutonian shore!*
> *Leave no black plume as a token of that lie thy soul hath spoken!*
> *Leave my loneliness unbroken!—quit the bust above my door!"*
> *Quoth the Raven, "Nevermore."*
> *And the Raven, never flitting, still is sitting, still is sitting*
> *On the pallid bust of Pallas just above my chamber door;*
> *And his eyes have all the seeming of a demon's that is dreaming,*
> *And the lamplight o'er him streaming throws his shadow on the floor;*
> *And my soul from out that shadow that lies floating on the floor*
> *Shall be lifted—nevermore!*

The pain felt by the poem's narrator came out of Poe's own personal experience. Three years earlier, his wife ruptured a blood vessel while singing and never regained her health. In a letter to a friend, Poe wrote about Virginia's illness:

Each time I felt all the agonies of her death—and at each accession of the disorder I loved her more dearly and clung to her life with more desperate pertinacity . . . I became insane, with long intervals of horrible sanity. During these fits of absolute unconsciousness I drank . . .

On June 29, 1847, Virginia Poe died at age 24, the same age at which Poe's mother had died. The love of beauty and the mourning of its passing into death was a theme that would haunt Poe's remaining poems and stories, particularly the beautiful poem "Annabel Lee." He began drinking more to drown his sorrows, and this made it harder and harder for him to find work. Although he was for a time owner and editor of the magazine *The Broadway Journal*, the publication soon went under from a lack of capital.

Poe's last years were a spiraling descent that he vainly struggled against. He wooed several women, hoping perhaps to find stability and financial security in a second marriage. But each engagement came to nothing, for whatever reasons. In late June 1849, Poe left his beloved Aunt Clemm in their squalid cottage outside of New York City and traveled to Richmond, which he considered his home. He arrived with two dollars in his pocket. In Richmond, he gave some lectures on literary criticism and reestablished his friendship with a woman who had jilted him years earlier when he was a university student. Her name was Elmira Shelton, and she was now a well-to-do widow. After a brief courtship, Poe proposed to her. Elmira seemed interested, but told him he'd have to wait for her answer.

In good spirits, Poe left on the train for Baltimore on September 27. He planned to return to New York, get his aunt and rush back to Richmond and his wedding.

What happened next remains a mystery to this day. Poe lingered in Baltimore longer than he intended. Some people reported seeing him at a lady friend's birthday party, where he was drinking heavily, but none of this can be substantiated. What we do know is that on October 3, a friend of Poe's in the city received this urgent note from a stranger.

Dear sir,

There is a gentleman, rather the worse for wear, at Ryan's 4th ward polls, who goes under the cognomen of Edgar A. Poe, and who appears in great distress, and he says he is acquainted with you, and I assure you, he is in need of immediate assistance.

The friend found Poe unconscious and rushed him to a hospital. He died there four days later, never fully regaining consciousness. His last words were reported to be, "Lord help my poor soul." The cause of death remains unknown.

Poe's death was given small space in the obituary pages. Incredibly, his own hand-picked literary executor, one Rufus Griswold, was also one of his bitterest enemies! Griswold misrepresented Poe's life and work in a devastating biography that ruined his reputation for years to come. It led to many of the misconceptions about the author that remain even today. Time and new scholarship have helped to return Poe to where he belongs—in the forefront of American authors.

Today, Poe's fame rests primarily on his horror tales and a handful of masterful poems. While he was an astute critic, his criticism and literary principles have been surpassed by later writers. His criticism, however, did set new standards in American literature and helped to encourage its serious acceptance both at home and abroad.

The intensity of Poe's nightmarish vision, the sense of disturbing reality he gives to the most fantastic experiences, makes his tales chillingly memorable. We, his readers, suffer the cruel tortures of the Spanish Inquisition along with the helpless narrator of "The Pit and the Pendulum." We enter the mad world of the murderer in "The Tell-Tale Heart" and watch with horror as Roderick Usher goes to his doom in "The Fall of the House of Usher."

Poe's interest in horror and the imagination was reflected in the work of Nathaniel Hawthorne and Herman Melville. Melville was partly inspired by Poe's *Arthur Pym* when he wrote his masterpiece, *Moby-Dick*. Not only was Poe the father of the detective story and the horror tale, but he also influenced future writers of science fiction and modern authors who further explored the human psyche, such as another Southern gentleman, William Faulkner. The decay and moral corruption that Poe charted in his fiction was a major theme for Faulkner and other Southern writers in this century.

Perhaps the best description of Poe's genius comes from his own pen, when he describes the spirits who revel at Prince Prospero's castle in the story "The Masque of the Red Death": "There were much of the beautiful, much of the wanton, much of the *bizarre*, something of the terrible, and not a little of that which might have excited disgust."

Chronology

January 19, 1809   born in Boston, Massachusetts

1811   mother dies, goes to live with foster parents John and Frances Allan

1815–1820   lives in England with foster parents

1826   enters University of Virginia

1827   leaves college, enlists in Army; first book, *Tamberlane and Other Poems*, appears

1829   discharged honorably from Army

1830   briefly attends West Point Military Academy

1832   first five short stories published in magazines

1836   hired as editor of *Southern Literary Messenger*

1836   marries cousin Virginia Clemm

1838   only novel, *The Narrative of Arthur Gordon Pym*, appears

1840   *Tales of the Grotesque and Arabesque* published, including some of his most famous stories

1845   *The Raven and Other Poems* appears

1847   Virginia dies of tuberculosis

October 7, 1849   dies in Baltimore, Maryland under mysterious circumstances

Further Reading

Poe's Works

The Complete Stories of Edgar Allan Poe (Garden City, N.Y.: Doubleday, 1966). This comprehensive volume contains all the tales and the little-read but fascinating, *The Narrative of Arthur Gordon Pym*.

The Mentor Book of Major American Poets (New York: New American Library, 1962, paper). This anthology contains a good selection of Poe's poetry, including "The Raven." Whitman and Dickinson are also well represented.

Books About Edgar Allan Poe

Lettice Cooper, *The Young Edgar Allan Poe* (New York: Roy Publishers, 1964). An interesting, though largely fictionalized life of the author, from early childhood to age 18.

Julian Symons, *The Tell-Tale Heart: The Life and Work of Edgar Allan Poe* (New York; Harper & Row, 1978). A good, thorough biography and critical study by a well-known mystery writer.

Nathaniel Hawthorne: The Haunted Writer

Nathaniel Hawthrone toiled at his writing for over 20 years before becoming famous "overnight" with the publication of The Scarlet Letter. This photograph was taken a few years before his death in 1864.
(Library of Congress)

---

*I*n 1692, one of the darkest events in American history took place in the colonial town of Salem, Massachusetts. A group of young girls, claiming to be tormented by Satan, began to accuse their neighbors of being Satan's helpmates—witches. The Puritan authorities believed them, and scores of innocent people were put on trial for witchcraft. Before the hysteria ended, 19 people were hanged and one poor man was "pressed" to death under heavy weights.

One of the three presiding judges in the infamous Salem witch trials was John Hathorne. Later, Hathorne, along with other officials involved, would come to regret his rash deeds. The Hathornes remained in Salem, but their fortunes gradually declined. Many years later, this would lead Judge Hathorne's great-grandson to wonder if perhaps the family, and the town, wasn't somehow cursed by God himself for its sins.

A dark sense of guilt haunted this sensitive young man and would compel him to write the first great American novel and a score of masterful stories. The young man, who would add a letter to his name, perhaps to escape from the family curse, was Nathaniel Hawthorne.

The Salem that Hawthorne was born into on July 4, 1804, was no longer the thriving town and prosperous seaport it had once been. It was entering a slow decline that would be hastened by the opening of the Erie Canal in the 1830s. The canal effectively ended Salem's importance as a trading port.

Hawthorne's father was a sea captain, who died in a foreign land of yellow fever when Nathaniel was only four. His mother Elizabeth was left grief-stricken and moved into her father's house in Salem with her son and two daughters. Here she remained a virtual recluse for 40 years, until her death.

The family homestead was a dark and lonely place for a growing boy, but Hawthorne didn't seem to mind. He loved the musty old books in the library and read the English writer John Bunyan's *Pilgrim's Progress* when he was only six. This symbolic tale of man's journey through a sinful world was to become his favorite book. A leg injury at nine confined Hawthorne to the house for two years, which didn't bother him in the least. It only left him more time to read and think. At 16, already a budding writer, he wrote a weekly newspaper for his own amusement.

The following year, Hawthorne entered the freshman class of Bowdoin College in Maine. Among his classmates was an ambitious young man from New Hampshire, Franklin Pierce, who would play a major role in Hawthorne's career. Hawthorne was a strikingly handsome but shy college student. He had an impressive large head, thick, dark hair, brooding eyebrows and deep blue eyes that, according to one friend, flashed fire. At Bowdoin, he became convinced he wanted to be a writer. In a letter to his mother he wrote:

I do not want to be a doctor and live by men's diseases; nor a minister, to live by their sins; nor a lawyer and live by their quarrels. So I don't see that there is anything left for me but to be an author.

In 1825, upon graduation, Hawthorne returned home to Salem, where, as critic Malcolm Cowley observed, he "disappeared like a stone dropped in a well." Hawthorne holed up in the family homestead with his books and his thoughts and did not emerge for 12 long years. During this time he lived like a monk. He wrote and read in his top-story bedroom all day, his meals left outside his closed door. He never ventured outside except after dark, when he would go for long walks through the deserted streets of Salem like a wandering ghost. He had few friends and remained a topic of gossip for the townsfolk.

Hawthorne wrote stories and sketches furiously during these years. When they were repeatedly rejected by publishers, he burned them in frustration. Finally, in 1828, he finished a novel, *Fanshawe*, which he paid to have published privately. When the novel failed to sell well, he felt ashamed and attempted to buy up as many copies as possible. But *Fanshawe* had at least one admiring reader, a Boston publisher named Samuel Goodrich. Goodrich encouraged Hawthorne to continue writing. In 1830, the hermit of Salem published his first stories in a local newspaper, the Salem *Gazette*. Soon after, Goodrich published his story, "Young Provincial" in his annual gift-book, *The Token*.

What Hawthorne sought now was a steady literary job. In 1836, he was hired to edit the strangely titled *American Magazine of Useful and Entertaining Knowledge* in Boston. He was promised a salary of $500 a year, but ended up receiving only $20 for all his hard work. Like Edgar Allan Poe, Hawthorne was quickly learning the difficulties of trying to make a living in the magazine trade.

The next year, however, his first volume of short stories, *Twice-Told Tales*, was published. In a preface to the book, Hawthorne, always the model of modesty, referred to himself as "the obscurest man of letters in America." In a letter to a former classmate from Bowdoin, Henry Wadsworth Longfellow, Hawthorne looked back on his years of self-imposed solitude:

By some witchcraft or order . . . I have been carried apart from the main current of life, and find it impossible to get back again . . . I have made a captive of myself and put me into a dungeon, and now I cannot find the key to let myself out—and if the door were open, I should be almost afraid to come out.

But out of obscurity Hawthorne would finally emerge. Longfellow, who was already gaining fame as a poet, read *Twice-Told Tales* and gave it a favorable review. He felt that here was a new and distinct voice in American literature.

Most of Hawthorne's stories were set in the Puritan past of his native state. Like Poe, he wrote of dark and foul deeds, and sometimes the supernatural entered into his tales. But unlike Poe, Hawthorne focused more on the effects of sin and guilt than on the evil acts themselves.

The most famous story from the collection, "The Minister's Black Veil," for example, is about a respected Puritan minister who inexplicably appears before his congregation one day wearing a black veil over his face. He spends the rest of his life with his face covered, and even in death the townspeople honor his request to leave it so. What sin or monstrous grief caused the minister to do this is never revealed, but the veil as a symbol for man's hidden self is hauntingly powerful. It would be the first of many potent symbols that Hawthorne would skillfully weave into his stories and novels.

Hawthorne's Salem neighbors were surprised to suddenly find a literary celebrity in their midst. Foremost among his admirers was Elizabeth Peabody, an intellectual young woman who befriended the shy author and introduced him to her cultured circle of friends. Among these was her invalid sister, Sophia. When Hawthorne met Sophia, he fell instantly in love. Although they would not be married for nearly five years, Hawthorne considered her his inspiration and referred to her as his "sole companion."

Although his talent as a writer was recognized by thoughtful readers, the greater world knew little yet of Nathaniel Hawthorne. He turned to politics to find a job that would pay the bills. A staunch Democrat, Hawthorne received a political appointment to the Boston Custom House in 1839. His job was to weigh and gauge salt, coal and other incoming goods. It was tedious, painstaking work, and Hawthorne soon grew to hate it. After two years, he left the Custom House and decided to look for a new life for himself and his soon-to-be bride.

Hawthorne's friends and literary acquaintances had started an unusual community in Massachusetts called Brook Farm. Brook Farm was a noble experiment in communal living that attempted to mix honest manual labor with the intellectual life. Farm chores alternated with lectures and classes in philosophy and literature. But communal life did not agree with the solitary Hawthorne, and the optimistic social viewpoint it promoted ran against his more fatalistic grain. In a letter to Sophia he wrote, ". . . a man's soul may be buried and perish under a dung-heap or in the furrows of a field, just as well as under a pile of money." For him, a rural paradise was no cure for the illnesses that beset America's growing materialism. Hawthorne left the community after spending less than a year there. Brook Farm collapsed after eight years.

In 1842, Hawthorne and Sophia were married and moved to Concord, Massachusetts. Concord was a center of intellectual and cultural life in New England. It was home to the poet and philosopher Ralph Waldo Emerson, writer Henry David Thoreau and social reformer Bronson Alcott. The young couple moved into the Old Manse, a roomy old house where Hawthorne wrote his next collection of tales, appropriately entitled *Mosses from an Old Manse.*

Paying the rent for the Old Manse on a writer's meager income soon proved impossible, however, and the Hawthornes moved back to Salem and his mother's house in 1845. Again, his political connections won him a job, this time in the Salem Custom House. Hawthorne detested the work as much as he had in Boston. When a change in administrations released him from his position, he was only temporarily upset. "God bless my enemies, say I," he later wrote. "If it had not been for their kind services, I might have been in the Surveyor's Room this day!"

Instead, he returned to writing. A story he had written years before involving an adulteress had given him an idea for a novel. But with a wife and now two children to support, Hawthorne wondered if he would ever finish it. One day in 1849, the publisher James T. Fields visited Hawthorne. Seeing the author's depressed state, Fields offered to publish anything he wrote. Hawthorne immediately gave him the outline of his novel and promised to flesh it out. With renewed enthusiasm, Hawthorne finished the novel and read it to his wife. "It broke her heart," he wrote, "and sent her to bed with a grievous headache,—which I look upon as a triumphant success."

The novel, *The Scarlet Letter*, was published in 1850 and sold 5,000 copies in just ten days. Upon reading it, Washington Irving, the grand old man of American letters, cried, "Masterly! Masterly!" Thousands of readers since have agreed with his judgment. *The Scarlet Letter* is considered Hawthorne's greatest work and one of the masterpieces of American literature. After 25 years of struggle, Nathaniel Hawthorne, at 46, was a famous and successful author.

The plot of *The Scarlet Letter* is deceptively simple. In 17th-century Boston, Hester Prynne, a Puritan maiden, creates a scandal by giving birth to a child out of wedlock. The authorities demand she reveal the name of the man responsible, but Hester refuses. For the sin of adultery she is forced to wear the letter "A" in red, embroidered on her dress. Hester's husband, an aged doctor named Roger Chillingworth, arrives from Europe and vows vengeance on the man responsible. Chillingworth correctly suspects that Arthur Dimmesdale, a rising young minister, is the guilty party. He befriends the clergyman, all the while gloating over and adding to the tormented man's burden of guilt. Hester plans to escape with Dimmesdale and their daughter, Pearl, to England, but Chillingworth hears of their plan and foils it. In the brilliant climax, Dimmesdale reveals his guilt amid a public ceremony, releasing him from his sin and Chillingworth's power. He dies, redeemed at last, in Hester's arms.

Unlike James Fenimore Cooper, his great contemporary, Hawthorne was a meticulous craftsman. Every element of the novel is carefully conceived. Atmosphere, setting, characters and symbolism all mesh together to create a work of breathtaking power. Despite its distant setting and Hawthorne's somewhat antiquated language, the novel reads as well today as when it was first published.

Perhaps what stands out the most is Hawthorne's masterful use of symbols. Each of the three central characters works as both a full-blooded person and a symbol. Chillingworth is the mind—cold, calculating, scientific and ultimately evil. Dimmesdale is the spirit—strong, other-worldly, but weakened by sin and its resulting guilt. Hester is the force of love, which finally overcomes both the mind and spirit. The most apparent symbol of all is the scarlet letter itself. Hawthorne weaves it in and out of his tale in a hundred variations. At one point, Dimmesdale sees the A formed in the sky by a shower of stars like some terrible omen from heaven. At the climax, he tears open his garments to reveal the letter etched on his very breast, a sign of his hidden guilt.

The novel is structured like a symphony, with each character given his or her own movement. The cold, Puritan community is symbolized by the ever-present scaffold in the marketplace where Hester and her shame are first put on public display. The only escape for Hester, Pearl and Dimmesdale is the dark forest. Here God's love and the world of nature offer them a temporary sanctuary from the unforgiving world of men. Here is an excerpt from this section:

They sat down again, side by side, and hand clasped in hand, on the mossy trunk of the fallen tree. Life had never brought them a gloomier hour; it was the point whither their pathway had so long been tending, and darkening ever, as it stole along;—and yet it inclosed a charm that made them linger upon it, and claim another, and another, and, after all, another moment. The forest was obscure around them, and creaked with a blast that was passing through it. The boughs were tossing heavily above their heads; while one solemn old tree groaned dolefully to another, as if telling the sad story of the pair that sat beneath, or constrained to forebode evil to come.

And yet they lingered. How dreary looked the forest-track that led backward to the settlement, where Hester Prynne must take up again the burden of her ignominy, and the minister the hollow mockery of his good name! So they lingered an instant longer. No golden light had ever been so precious as the gloom of this dark forest. Here, seen only by his eyes, the scarlet letter need not burn into the bosom of the fallen woman! Here, seen only by her eyes, Arthur Dimmesdale, false to God and man, might be, for one moment, true!

The success of *The Scarlet Letter* opened the floodgates of Hawthorne's creativity. In the next three years, he wrote five books. The first of these was a second novel, *The House of the Seven Gables*. In this book, Hawthorne continued his exploration into guilt and redemption, this time through the dark past of the Pyncheon family of New England. Hawthorne drew on the Salem witch trials and his own family history for inspiration. Another novel, *The Blithedale Romance*, was modeled after Brook Farm and his experiences there. He also wrote two children's books, still read today, and a campaign biography of his old friend Franklin Pierce, who was running for president.

In the election of 1852, Pierce, a Democrat, defeated the Whig Party candidate Winfield Scott, to become the 14th president of

The House of the Seven Gables, in Salem, Massachusetts, shown here, inspired Hawthorne's famous novel of the same name. Today the house is a museum dedicated to the author and his work.
(The House of the Seven Gables Settlement Association)

the United States. Pierce's administration reads like a Hawthorne tale. Two months before his inauguration, Pierce's 11-year-old son died in a railroad accident. His wife, overcome with grief, was a recluse for nearly two years and was called "the shadow in the White House." Growing bitterness over the issue of slavery further troubled President Pierce. His support of the rights of new immigrants angered members of his own party and assured that he would not serve another term.

Pierce's administration, however, did bode well for Hawthorne. The new president appointed his friend U.S. consul to England. The Hawthornes ended up spending seven years in Europe, dividing most of their time between England and Italy. While Hawthorne enjoyed Europe and its cultural riches, he found little of the inspiration there that Irving and Cooper had before him. He completed only one major work during his time abroad, a novel, *The Marble Faun*. This intriguing and underrated book traces the lives of two American artists in Rome.

In 1859, fever nearly claimed the life of Hawthorne's eldest daughter, Una, and he himself became seriously ill. The following year the family returned to America, where Hawthorne's health continued to decline. Exhausted and sick, he started several works, but was unable to finish any of them. The books he later did complete proved inferior to his earlier work. As the Civil War broke out, Hawthorne felt more and more alienated by the rapidly changing world around him. He found it impossible to write about contemporary America, which he complained was all sunlight without shadows.

In May 1864, two months before his 60th birthday, Hawthorne started on a trip with his friend Pierce to the White Mountains of New Hamsphire. He hoped the fresh air would revive his spirits. In Plymouth, New Hampshire the two men stopped overnight at an inn. During the night, Pierce entered his friend's room to check on him and discovered Hawthorne had stopped breathing.

Hawthorne's funeral was attended by many of the leading writers of the day. The manuscript of *The Dolliver Romance*, the novel he was working on at the time of his death, was laid upon his coffin. Later Emerson wrote, "There was a tragic element in the painful solitude of the man, which, I suppose, could not long be endured and he died of it."

Nathaniel Hawthorne's reputation has not diminished over the years. Although he was far from prolific, his four novels and 100 stories have stood the test of time. He built his books like a master architect builds a building, with attention to every detail and a clear vision of the overall design. This concentration on form had an immense influence on such later American novelists as Henry James.

Hawthorne was also the first American author to master the use of symbols in his work. Symbolism is never forced on his characters or stories but arises naturally from them, enriching the themes and meaning of his work. His symbolism influenced many younger writers, none perhaps so profoundly as Herman Melville, who was a neighbor and friend when Hawthorne lived in Lenox, Massachusetts. Melville's own greatest symbol, the white whale in *Moby-Dick*, was developed out of long discussions with the older writer.

Finally, Hawthorne's deep sense of morality made him as great a social critic of American society as Cooper or Thoreau. The greatest sin for Hawthorne was not immorality but intellectual pride. This theme comes through clearly in such fine stories as "Rappaccini's Daughter" and "The Birthmark." In both these tales proud men of science end up destroying the people they most love due to their blind devotion to knowledge. Unless man's sense of moral responsibility and his capacity for love keeps up with his ability to create new technology, Hawthorne seems to be saying, only disaster can await us. In these days of nuclear bombs and the potential of world annihilation, his message is more relevant than ever.

Chronology

July 4, 1804   born in Salem, Massachusetts

1825   graduates from Bowdoin College in Maine

1828   first novel, *Fanshawe*, published

1837   *Twice-Told Tales*, first story collection, appears

1842   marries Sophia Peabody and moves to Old Manse in Concord

1846–49   works in the Salem Custom House as surveyor

1850   *The Scarlet Letter* published

1851   *The House of the Seven Gables* published; moves with family to Lenox, Massachusetts

1852   *The Blithedale Romance* published; friend Franklin Pierce becomes President

1853   appointed U.S. consul to England

1857   moves to Italy, where he writes *The Marble Faun*

1860   returns to America

May 19, 1864   dies in sleep at inn in Plymouth, New Hampshire, en route to the White Mountains

Further Reading

Hawthorne's Works

The Birthmark and Other Stories (New York: Scholastic, 1968, paper). A good collection for young adults, followed by notes and a biographical sketch.

The House of the Seven Gables (Pleasantville, N.Y.: Reader's Digest, 1985). A beautiful edition of Hawthorne's classic novel with marvelous woodcut illustrations by David Frampton.

The Portable Hawthorne, edited by Malcolm Cowley (New York: Penguin, 1977). An excellent introduction to Hawthorne's work and life, includes the complete novel *The Scarlet Letter*, 13 stories and selections from his notebooks, journals and letters.

Books About Nathaniel Hawthorne

Nina Baym, *The Scarlet Letter: A Reading* (Boston: Twayne, 1986). An excellent critical companion to Hawthorne's masterpiece especially written for young adults, a part of Twayne's Masterwork Studies series.

Terrence Martin, *Nathaniel Hawthorne* (Boston: Twayne, 1983). A good critical introduction to the writer's fiction and his major themes.

Mark Van Doren, *Nathaniel Hawthorne* (New York: William Sloane, 1949). Excellent critical biography, part of the American Men of Letters Series.

Herman Melville: The Author Who Lived Among the Cannibals

Few writers have experienced the highs and lows that Herman Melville did in his career. Celebrated for his first five novels, his public deserted him after the publication of Moby-Dick, *his masterpiece. This portrait was taken before he gave up professional writing at age 37.*
(Library of Congress)

*O*n November 20, 1820, one of the worst disasters in sailing history took place in a remote part of the South Pacific Ocean. The whaling ship *Essex* was attacked by a mammoth sperm whale. The crazed creature rammed the three-masted vessel "with ten-fold fury and vengeance," first mate Owen Chase later said. The

47

crew abandoned the ship, which quickly sank, into smaller whale-boats. One by one the survivors succumbed to starvation and hardship, until only Chase and seven others were rescued more than 80 days later.

The *Essex* tragedy made headlines in every American newspaper at the time and lived on for generations in sea lore. It haunted the imagination of a young writer, Herman Melville. What fascinated Melville most was not the tragedy itself but survivor Chase's description of the killer whale's "horrid aspect and malignancy." He spoke of the creature as if it were evil incarnate. Melville decided to retell the *Essex*'s story in a novel. But he changed the whale's color to white and named him Moby-Dick, after Mocha-Dick, a legendary whale that also really lived. Thus, from an account in a newspaper came what many readers regard as the greatest of American novels.

Herman Melville was born on August 1, 1819, in New York City to a prosperous New England merchant and his wife, a member of one of New York's finest Dutch families. But life changed suddenly for the Melvilles when Herman was only 11. Allan Melville's business failed and he suffered a nervous breakdown. He died two years later, leaving his family of eight near poverty.

Herman, along with his brothers, went to work to help support the family. Barely 13, he tried a number of jobs. He sold hats in a store owned by one brother, worked in an uncle's bank and even taught school outside of Pittsfield, Massachusetts. But like many a youth faced with a dull, grim life on land, Melville turned to the sea for escape. At 19, he signed on as cabin boy on a merchant ship and sailed to Liverpool, England. He no sooner returned to America than he joined a whaling ship bound for the Pacific.

Whaling was a major industry in New England in the first half of the 19th century. Whaling ships set off from the island of Nantucket and New Bedford, Massachusetts by the hundreds to hunt and kill sperm whales for their fat, called blubber. The oil derived from blubber was used as a fuel for lamps, as a lubricant, and an ingredient for candles. *Ambergris*, a substance found in the whales' intestines, was used to make fine perfumes. From 1820 to 1850, American whaling ships killed some 10,000 whales every year.

The voyages of the whaling ships were often long and arduous. Life on board ship could be intolerable, especially if the captain was a stern taskmaster. Melville's captain was such a man, and when the whaler anchored at one of the Marquesas Islands in the South Pacific, he jumped ship with a friend. To escape capture, the two young men hid in a valley inhabited by a native tribe who were reported to be fierce cannibals. But to the sailors' surprise, the natives, called Typees, treated them with hospitality and kindness. Melville lived among the Typees for a month and then left the valley to join another whaler from Australia.

Once again, ship life proved too much to bear, and Melville deserted on the tropical island of Tahiti. This time he was captured and put in jail. He managed to escape and with a fellow prisoner explored a nearby island. He signed on a third whaling ship and finally ended up in the Sandwich Islands, which are known today as the Hawaiian Islands. In August 1843, Melville went aboard the Navy frigate *United States* as a seaman and returned to Boston just over a year later. He traveled from there to his mother's home in Albany, New York.

In a few short years Melville had experienced enough adventures to last him a lifetime. But what would he do now for a living? He decided to sit down and try to write a book about his experiences. He had good reason to believe such a book might sell well. The American reading public was fascinated by anything foreign or exotic. By the 1840s, the large Eastern cities of the United States were as settled and civilized as any metropolis in Europe. Life was becoming a little too boring, and urban Americans thrilled to the true accounts written by travelers and explorers of faraway places—places they could otherwise only dream about. Such early travel books became best-sellers.

Melville centered his story around his stay among the Typees three years earlier. He so skillfully mixed fact and fiction that the London publisher John Murray believed the novel to be a totally factual narrative. Murray published Melville's novel *Typee* in 1846. It immediately became a literary sensation. Melville became a celebrity and was known to the public as "the man who lived among the cannibals."

Although *Typee* was a well-told adventure tale and contained fascinating descriptions of life among the Polynesian natives, it also contained the seeds of a more serious theme. This theme was the corruption of innocence in a world of evil. For Melville, the Typees were innocents, living in a kind of Eden where good and evil were unknown. It was the white missionaries and traders who had brought corrupting civilization and a sense of sin to these child-like people. "Thrice happy are they who inhabiting some yet undiscovered island in the midst of the ocean, have never been brought into contaminating contact with the white man," he wrote.

But Melville's deeper ideas were lost on most of his readers, who were merely entertained by his adventurous tale. Encouraged by his success, Melville went on to mine his experiences on sea and land in his writing. His days in Tahiti were the basis for his second novel, *Omoo*. *Mardi* quickly followed as a sequel to *Omoo*, but midway through it, Melville the artist took over from Melville the spinner of tales. The book became a symbolic quest for truth in an immoral world. The public was bewildered and disappointed with the novel, and Melville quickly retreated back to the safer ground of high adventure. *Redburn* (1849) retold his first voyage to England, and *White-Jacket* (1850) was an imaginative account of his last voyage home around South America's Cape Horn.

These five books, written in quick succession, brought Melville wealth and fame and made him one of America's most popular writers. He married the daughter of the chief justice of Massachusetts, moved to New York City and toured Europe. On his return, he bought a farm in Pittsfield, Massachusetts and set down to write the story of a whaling voyage, inspired by the *Essex* tragedy.

Melville began *Moby-Dick* as another thrilling sea adventure. But then his path crossed with that of another author, and the

Arrowhead, shown here in 1862, was the farm in Pittsfield, Massachusetts where Melville lived for 14 years and wrote Moby-Dick *and other works. Hawthorne, a neighbor in nearby Lenox, often visited and was an important influence on* Moby-Dick.
(The Berkshire Atheneum)

book and Melville's life were changed forever. Nathaniel Hawthorne had recently moved to nearby Lenox after the success of *The Scarlet Letter*, and the two men met and became friends. Although Hawthorne was 15 years older, the writers had many things in common. Both were deeply introspective men who were fascinated by evil and its effects on human beings. They also shared a tragic vision of life that was at odds with the optimism that permeated their young nation. They would meet in Hawthorne's barn, stretch out on the hay and talk about everything under the sun, including the new book Melville was writing. Hawthorne encouraged the younger author to pursue the deeper, darker themes that were roiling in his mind. Melville followed this advice and transformed his sea adventure into an epic story of good and evil. He also infused it with the kind of symbolism and philosophical thought that Hawthorne's own work was fraught with.

Moby-Dick is the story of a great white whale that years earlier had taken the leg of the whaling captain Ahab. Ahab has vowed revenge on the whale and turns the whaling expedition of his ship, the *Pequod*, into a megalomaniac hunt for Moby-Dick. The story is told by Ishmael, a young sailor. The rest of the crew includes representatives of nearly every race and religion. The *Pequod* finally encounters its prey, and the entire ship and crew are destroyed by the whale, except for Ishmael, who lives to tell the tale.

As with Hawthorne's *Scarlet Letter*, Melville's masterpiece is enriched with symbolism and layers of meaning. Moby-Dick has been variously interpreted as evil in the world, knowledge and even reality itself. Ahab, obsessed with destroying evil, becomes the very thing he seeks to destroy. Ishmael, who is Everyman, survives the catastrophic battle because he, unlike most of the crew, rejects Ahab's obsession.

Melville endows his whale with a universal power as great as the sea it swims in. Here, Ishmael attempts to describe the meaning of the whale's whiteness after first seeing the creature:

It was the whiteness of the whale that above all things appalled me . . . Is it that by its indefiniteness it shadows forth the heartless voids and immensities of the universe, and thus stabs up from behind with the thought of annihilation, when beholding the white depths of the milky way? Or is it, that as in essence whiteness is not so much a color as the visible absence of color, and at the same time the concrete of all colors; is it for these reasons that there is such a dumb blankness, full of meaning, in a wide landscape of snows . . . And of all these things the Albino whale was the symbol. Wonder ye then at the fiery hunt?

This was a far cry from the simple adventures of *Typee* and *Omoo*. Melville had written no less than a masterpiece, and yet few readers at the time recognized this. The critics were befuddled by this burly, thorny epic. The literary establishment ridiculed it and the reading public largely ignored it.

Melville knew he had written a profound book, and he became angry and bitter. In response to the public's indifference, he wrote a dark satire about a young writer who becomes corrupted by the world and ends up destroying himself and the people he loves. *Pierre, or the Ambiguities* continued the study of evil Melville began in *Moby-Dick* in a very different style. There was no whale hunt or exotic adventure to draw in the reading public. The book was so strange and savage that it alienated the few readers that Melville had left.

Melville continued to write, but a near breakdown sapped his powers. His best writing during this time was a collection of short stories he called *The Piazza Tales*, published in 1856. A piazza is a large covered porch, the place where Melville wrote these tales. Two of them have become classics of the form. "Benito Cereno" is set aboard a slave ship where appearance and reality are deceptive. The captain, Benito Cereno, appears to be in control but is actually the prisoner of the slaves, whose ringleader poses as his servant. Evil operates under the guise of goodness and only the wise person can distinguish between the two, Melville is saying.

Equally memorable is "Bartleby the Scrivener," an intriguing tale of a scrivener, or copyist, who one day refuses to do any more work for the lawyer who employs him. To every demand he replies cryptically, "I should prefer not to." Bartleby refuses to leave the office and spends his days staring blankly at a wall. In desperation, the lawyer moves to a new office and Bartleby dies in prison. In this powerful allegory Melville is questioning our responsibility to our fellow humans and the impossibility of meaningful communication between people. The absurdity of the situation is startlingly modern and foreshadows the work of such 20th century writers as Samuel Beckett and Eugene Ionesco.

Unfortunately, Melville's stories met with no more success than his other mature works. Disillusioned and embittered, he gave up

These are Melville's four children—from left to right: Stanwix, Frances, Malcolm and Elizabeth. Malcolm, the eldest, committed suicide at home at age 18.
(The Berkshire Atheneum)

writing professionally at age 37. He sold his country farm and moved back to New York City. Here, one of America's greatest writers took a job as deputy inspector of customs for the Port of New York City. To support his family, he would remain in this stultifying job for 19 years.

During these years, Melville did not entirely abandon writing. He turned from the public forum of fiction to the more introspective world of poetry. He wrote now for himself and a few friends and published several volumes of poetry at his own expense. His most ambitious poem, *Clarel*, runs 10,000 lines and has been hailed by those few scholars who have read it as one of his finest achievements.

When Melville died on September 28, 1891, it caused hardly a ripple in the national press. The obituary in the New York *Press* read, "Probably, if the truth were known, even his own generation had long thought him dead, so quiet have been the later years of his life."

But in his last years of retirement. Melville had returned to writing prose and had written a long story that would rival *Moby-Dick* in its power. *Billy Budd* remained hidden away among Melville's papers at his death, and did not see the light of publication until 1924. The timing could not have been better. Three years earlier, critic R. M. Weaver had written the first biography of the writer, *Herman Melville, Mariner and Mystic*. It revived interest in the all-but-forgotten author, and by the 1940s Melville was internationally recognized as one of America's greatest writers.

Critic Maxwell Geismar has called *Billy Budd* "just about the best short story ever written." Billy, who Melville calls "a man child," is impressed, or forced, to serve on a British warship during a war with the French in 1798. Billy's simple goodness and handsome, boyish features make him a favorite among the rugged crew of the *Indomitable*. John Claggart, the ship's master-at-arms, however, is less impressed. Depicted as the embodiment of evil, Claggart plots to destroy Budd and the goodness he represents. When he falsely accuses Billy of treason before the captain, Edward Vere, a fatal stutter prevents Billy from defending himself with words. Instead, the youth strikes out with his fists and accidentally kills Claggart.

Vere realizes Claggart's villainy and sympathizes with Billy. At the same time, he comes to the awful realization that to maintain discipline and uphold military law in wartime, he must sentence Billy to death for killing an officer. "Struck dead by an angel of God!" Vere exclaims over Claggart's corpse. "Yet the angel must hang!"

Billy's trial and last night are beautifully rendered in Melville's rich prose. But the most moving passage is the description of his pre-dawn execution:

> *Billy stood facing aft. At the penultimate moment, his words, his only words, words wholly unobstructed in the utterance were these— "God bless Captain Vere!" Syllables so unanticipated coming from one with the ignominious hemp about his neck . . . with one voice from alow and aloft came a resonant sympathetic echo—"God bless Captain Vere!" And yet at that instant Billy alone must have been in their hearts, even as he was in their eyes.*

54

> *The hull deliberately recovering from the periodic roll to leeward was just regaining an even keel, when the last signal . . . was given. At the same moment it chanced that the vapory fleece hanging low in the East, was shot through with a soft glory as of the fleece of the Lamb of God seen in mystical vision, and simultaneously therewith, watched by the wedged mass of upturned faces, Billy ascended; and, ascending, took the full rose of the dawn.*

As innocent as the natives of Typee, Billy Budd could not survive in a flawed world made by men. Ironically, it is not Claggart's pure evil that condemns Billy, but the "good" Captain Vere, entrapped by the laws he must enforce.

The tragedy of Herman Melville's life mirrors the tragic sense of his work. He began his literary career as the man who lived among the cannibals, and ended it being devoured by the civilized "cannibals" of his own country, who treated him with far less mercy than the Typees. America, flushed by the excitement of western expansion, rejected the existence-of-evil in Melville's work, even as it was exterminating the Native Americans and gearing up to fight a bloody civil war over the old sin of black slavery.

Melville's best work was written both for its own time and for all time. Like his great mentor, Hawthorne, he used symbols and philosophical thought to plumb the depths of the human spirit and seek answers to that eternal question: "What is evil and why does it exist in the world?"

Unlike Hawthorne, Melville was not always a careful craftsman. Both *Moby-Dick* and *Billy Budd* are marred by intellectual digressions that interrupt the flow of the story and frustrate the modern reader. In *Moby-Dick* the reader learns everything he ever wanted to know about whaling and probably a lot more. But these very digressions show the vastness of Melville's mind, and his desire to encompass all of the world in his great epic.

Like Cooper, there was a self-destructive strain in the man. But where Cooper continued to throw himself into the fight of life, Melville withdrew from it into solitary darkness. Like Ahab, Melville may have looked "too long in the face of the unholy fire" and consumed himself with bitterness.

Melville's influence is as vast as the sea he loved. As a master of symbolism and psychological truth, he foreshadowed much of 20th-century literature. His preoccupation with the power of evil to corrupt has been continued by American novelists from Theodore Dreiser to William Faulkner. Melville's decision to forsake exploring exotic isles for the deeper exploration of the inner self was one that, in the end, cost him dearly. However, American literature has been all the richer for it.

Chronology

August 1, 1819	born in New York City
1831	father dies, family moves to Albany, New York
1837	sails on first sea voyage as cabin boy on merchant ship
1838–44	experiences many adventures in South Seas on various voyages
1847	*Typee*, first novel, establishes his reputation
1851	*Moby-Dick* published
1853	*Pierre* appears
1856	*The Piazza Tales*, including "Bartleby the Scrivener" and "Benito Cereno" published; gives up writing career at 37
1864	sells Pittsfield farm and moves to New York City
1866	appointed deputy inspector of customs for the Port of New York, job he holds for 19 years
September 28, 1891	dies in New York City
1921	*Herman Melville, Mariner and Mystic* by R. M. Weaver published, beginning a reevaluation of Melville's work
1924	*Billy Budd* published nearly 40 years after it is written

Further Reading

Melville's Works

Moby-Dick (New York: W.W Norton, 1967). This Norton Critical Edition of the classic novel contains reviews, criticisms and letters by the author, as well as a glossary of nautical terms.

Redburn (Garden City, N.Y.: Doubleday Anchor, paper, 1957). Melville's fourth novel is based largely on the author's first voyage to England as a sailor.

Billy Budd and Typee (New York: Washington Square Press, 1964, paper). This one volume contains Melville's first and last work, with the author's original introductions.

Books About Herman Melville

Richard Chase, editor. *Melville: A Collection Of Critical Essays* (Englewood Cliffs, N.J.: Prentice-Hall, 1962). Essays on the author and his important works, including contributions by critics and writers, part of 20th Century Interpretations series.

Jean Gould, *Young Mariner Melville* (New York: Dodd, Mead, 1956). Well-researched young-adult biography that makes good use of the author's letters and other writings; deals mostly with his life at sea.

Tyrus Hillway, *Herman Melville* (Boston: Twayne, 1979). A brief, but good introduction to his life and work, part of Twayne's U.S. Authors Series.

Charlotte E. Keyes, *High on the Mainmast: The Life of Herman Melville* (New College University Press, 1966). Another young-adult biography, especially strong on Melville's early years.

Kerry McSweeney, *Moby-Dick: Ishmael's Mighty Book* (Boston: Twayne, 1986). An excellent critical guide to reading Melville's masterpiece; part of Twayne Masterwork Studies series.

Henry David Thoreau:
The Genius of the Wood

Henry David Thoreau published only two books in all his all-too-short lifetime, but the second, Walden, *has become an American classic. This sketch by Samuel Rowse captures the sensitivity and inner serenity of the author.*
(The Thoreau Society)

*O*ne March day in 1845, a 28-year-old man surprised his neighbors in Concord, Massachusetts, by tramping off into the woods with an axe he borrowed from a friend. He chopped down a number of trees and built a small, one-room cabin for himself along the shore of Walden Pond. On Independence Day, this strange young man moved into his tiny cabin and lived there alone for two years and two months. Why? "I went to the woods because I wanted to live deliberately," he later wrote, "to front only the essential facts of life, and see if I could not learn what it had to teach, and not, when I came to die, discover that I had not lived . . . I wanted to live deep and suck out all the marrow of life . . . to know it by experience, and be able to give a true account of it . . ."

The young man was Henry David Thoreau, and the "true account" of his time in the woods has become one of the great works of American literature. Thoreau wrote no novels or stories, and precious few poems in his lifetime, but his importance as a writer and thinker rivals any other writer in 19th-century America.

Thoreau was born in the village of Concord, 20 miles west of Boston, on July 12, 1817. At the time, 2,000 people lived in Concord, most of them farmers. Although Thoreau would travel to New York, Maine and, late in life, as far west as Minnesota, Concord and its surrounding countryside would remain the center of his world. He grew to know every plant, bird and animal around Concord. The world of nature was the inspiration for his life and art.

The Thoreaus were a hardworking but hardly prosperous family. Henry's father, John, owned a small pencil factory, and his mother took in boarders to help make ends meet. Thoreau had two sisters and an older brother, John Jr., whom he was close to. Together the two boys built a small boat, and in it, enthusiastically explored the Concord River.

Thoreau loved the outdoors and such sports as swimming and hiking. His athletic, short, muscular body was offset by his large, scholarly nose and thoughtful, gray-blue eyes. At age ten, he wrote his first essay, entitled "The Seasons." All his life, Thoreau would be a keen student of the changing seasons, and would celebrate in his writing the natural wonders of fall, winter, spring and summer.

His parents were impressed by their son's intelligence and sent him to Concord Academy, the finest school in town. Here, Thoreau studied Greek and Latin. He would later master both and be able to read the great sagas of Homer and other ancient writers in the original. Through great sacrifice, the Thoreaus sent Henry to Harvard College, where he entered the class of 1833 at 16.

Thoreau was a good student at Harvard, but did not stand out among his more ambitious classmates. He was more interested in learning for learning's sake than for using knowledge to get ahead in the world with a profession. A new philosophy, originally from Germany, was sweeping across New England, and several of Thoreau's professors were followers of it. This philosophy expressed the discontentment of such writers as Hawthorne and Melville with the materialism that was becoming more and more a part of American life. It was a philosophy that encouraged people to turn away from the money-making business of the world and cultivate the inner world of the mind and spirit. It called on individuals to "transcend" their everyday lives and raise their consciousness by intellectual study and the study of nature. For these reasons, it came to be called Transcendentalism.

The leader of the Transcendentalists was a former Unitarian minister turned writer and speaker named Ralph Waldo Emerson. Emerson moved to Concord in the early 1830s, where he wrote many of the essays that would change the way American intellectuals thought about themselves and the world. In 1837, Emerson delivered his famous address on "The American Scholar" to Thoreau's graduating class at Harvard. It would have a profound effect on the young graduate. In the years ahead, Emerson would play an important role in Thoreau's life as friend, mentor and father figure.

Thoreau himself spoke at his graduation, along with other students. In his address he made the startling suggestion that every person work only one day a week and then spend the remaining six days enjoying the "sublime revelations of nature." Although such advice may have sounded ridiculous to the future lawyers, businessman and scholars in his class, Thoreau himself tried to live by it. As he later wrote, "If a man does not keep pace with his companions, perhaps it is because he hears a different drummer. Let him step to the music which he hears, however measured or far away."

Thoreau's "drummer" led him back to Concord, where, like many a young man with intellectual ambitions, he tried teaching. New England's public schools were far superior to those in other parts of the country, but they were not advanced by modern standards. Discipline was a major part of the curriculum, and students who misbehaved were flogged or whipped regularly. Young Thoreau abhorred physical punishment and found it went against everything he believed in. When school officials criticized him for being too lenient, he lined up six of his most troublesome students, flogged them roundly and then handed in his resignation.

Thoreau decided to set up his own private school and teach the way he wanted to. His small academy, which he ran with his brother John, was decades ahead of its time in its progressive approach to education. In his school, textbooks weren't as important as experience. Students were encouraged to think for themselves, and the class often took "field trips" to the country, to study nature and the region's early history. Such things were unheard of in more conventional public schools.

Meanwhile, Henry and John were taking their own field trips. They built a sailboat they called the *Musketaquid*, the Indian name for the Concord River. On their summer vacation they took a memorable voyage down the Concord and into the larger Merrimack River. Thoreau would later immortalize their trip in his first book, *A Week on the Concord and Merrimack Rivers*.

Their school might have prospered for years, if John hadn't taken ill. Henry decided the school was too much for him to manage alone, and he closed it down. He explored other ways to work that were less time-consuming and would meet his modest needs. He worked part-time in the family pencil factory, surveyed land for his neighbors and worked as a handyman. Most of his time he spent tramping the woods and fields, studying plants and animals and jotting down notes on everything he saw.

One day he walked 40 miles to Boston and back just to hear Emerson deliver a lecture. Soon after, he met the great man in Concord. Emerson was as impressed with Thoreau—14 years his junior—as Thoreau was with him. "I delight much in my young friend," he later wrote, "who seems to have as free and erect a mind as any I have ever met."

Emerson introduced Thoreau to some of his Transcendentalist friends, such as editor and writer Margaret Fuller and philosopher Bronson Alcott. He also encouraged Thoreau to keep a daily journal of his observations, thoughts and feelings. Thoreau took the advice and wrote religiously in his journal until a few years before his death. Thoreau's *Journals* were to be the great literary work of his life, out of which all his other books were to spring. When they were published after his death, they filled 39 volumes.

Emerson also made Thoreau a job offer he couldn't refuse. He suggested Thoreau move into his house as a combination handyman and caretaker. Emerson was often away on long lecture tours, and Thoreau would take care of things while he was gone. With his room and board provided, Thoreau was now free to study nature and write to his heart's content. It was an ideal arrangement.

During this time Thoreau's path crossed with another great writer. Nathaniel Hawthorne and his wife moved to Concord and met Thoreau at Emerson's home. When Thoreau's brother died of tetanus from a cut on a rusty nail in January 1842, the heartbroken man sold their sailboat to Hawthorne and taught the author how to sail it. While they became friends, Hawthorne's first impression of Thoreau was anything but flattering. ". . . he is long-nosed, queer-mouthed, and with uncouth and somewhat rustic manners," he wrote in his notebook. "He has repudiated all regular means of getting a living and seems inclined to lead a sort of Indian life."

Rustic though he might be, Thoreau was starting to make his mark as a writer. His poems and articles appeared in the Transcendentalist magazine, *The Dial*, which he even edited while Emerson was away. A job tutoring Emerson's brother's son in Staten Island brought Thoreau to New York City in 1843. He hoped to make connections in publishing there and find literary work. But Thoreau loathed New York, with its crowded streets and maddening pace. He found none of the joy and excitement there that had inspired earlier authors and his great contemporary, Walt Whitman. Homesick, he soon returned to Concord.

Not long after, Thoreau built his cabin on the shore of his beloved Walden Pond. The move to Walden was the culmination of everything Thoreau believed in. Here, he felt he could live as simply as modern man could, with few possessions and no commitments to the outside world. He would be free to confront "the great facts of his existence" by living close to nature.

Life on Walden Pond, however, was no summer vacation. Thoreau spent his days working hard. He planted and tended two acres of vegetables (he ate no meat), fished in the pond, cut firewood for his stove and plastered his rude cabin to insulate it from the oncoming winter. In the evenings he read and studied, wrote in his journal and toiled tirelessly on the manuscripts that would become his first two books. Sometimes, for entertainment, he played his flute.

Thoreau did not lead the life of a hermit, as many people suppose. He had many visitors to his cabin, ranging from his poet friend Ellery Channing to the local children on their way to pick berries in the woods. He walked into the village several times a

Walden Pond, where Thoreau lived from 1845 to 1847, is today a state park. The stone posts and chain mark the site where his cabin stood. The pond can be seen in the background. The pile of stones is a memorial; each stone was left by a visitor to the site.
(Brad Parker)

week to visit his parents, hear the latest gossip and buy the few groceries he needed. He boasted that his food budget was 27 cents a week.

Walden, the book that Thoreau wrote about his "life in the woods," is unlike anything else in American literature. It is a nature book, a journal, an autobiography and a collection of wise sayings and pithy thoughts all rolled into one. It is, above all, a book about one man's inner life and how he is changed by experience. By stripping his life down to the essentials, Thoreau came to recognize the true meaning of life in all its mystery and beauty. He skillfully drew on the everyday reality of his life to illuminate the greatest profundities of existence. Here are two good examples:

Time is but the stream I go a-fishing in. I drink at it; but while I drink I see the sandy bottom and detect how shallow it is. Its thin current slides away, but eternity remains. I would drink deeper; fish in the sky, whose bottom is pebbly with stars.

The mass of men lead lives of quiet desperation. What is called resignation is confirmed desperation. From the desperate city you go into the desperate country, and have to console yourself with the bravery of minks and muskrats. A stereotyped but unconscious despair is concealed even under what are called the games and amusements of mankind. There is no play in them, for this comes after work. But it is a characteristic of wisdom not to do desperate things.

This rich, beautifully balanced prose did not come easily. Thoreau labored on his sentences with the same careful craftsmanship with which he built his cabin or planned his bean garden.

One day in his second year at Walden, Thoreau went into town to have a shoe mended. He was stopped by his friend, the local jailkeeper, Sam Staples. Staples told Thoreau that he had not paid his poll tax of $1.50 and that, unless he did so at once, he would regretfully have to arrest him. Staples offered to loan Thoreau the money if he didn't have it, but Thoreau refused. It wasn't the tax itself that he objected to, but where the tax money was going.

The United States had recently gone to war with Mexico. While many Americans supported the war, Thoreau and others saw it as a war of imperialism, in which the United States wanted to grab up Mexican territory in the southwest. Worse still, there was reason to believe that once this land became part of the United States, slavery would be allowed to exist there.

Slavery was a major issue in the United States in the 1840s. It was banned in many Northern states, but still existed in the South. Whether slavery would be allowed in the new Western states and territories was a burning question that was dividing the nation. It would eventually lead to civil war.

Thoreau was strongly opposed to slavery, and had even given shelter at his Walden cabin to runaway slaves on their way to Canada and freedom. For all these reasons, Thoreau would not pay his poll tax and support a war and an institution he felt was wrong. So, in protest, he spent the night in the Concord jail. Thoreau wrote about his night in jail and the reasons that brought him there in an essay that would later come to be called "Civil

Disobedience." In this excerpt, he states why a person has a right, and duty, to disobey laws he believes wrongful:

How does it become a man to behave toward this American government to-day? I answer, that he cannot without disgrace be associated with it. I cannot for an instant recognize that political organization as my government which is the slave's government also . . . Unjust laws exist: shall we be content to obey them, or shall we endeavor to amend them, and obey them until we have succeeded, or shall we transgress them at once? . . . Moreover, any man more right than his neighbors constitutes a majority of one . . .

If a law is wrong, claimed Thoreau, people have the right to break that law, in order, by their example, to draw attention to it and change it. This was a revolutionary idea in 1846. But "Civil Disobedience" would become required reading for such great social leaders of the 20th century as India's Mahatma Gandhi and America's Martin Luther King. Both men would follow Thoreau's example and win justice for their peoples through nonviolent, peaceful protest.

Thoreau unwillingly left jail the next morning, when one of his aunts paid his poll tax for him. But when he left his Walden retreat on September 6, 1847, it was completely voluntary. He wrote that he felt he might have "several more lives to live," and it was time to move on.

Certainly, one of these lives was that of the professional writer. Through his writing, Thoreau hoped to share his wisdom and experience with other people. In May 1849, a Boston publisher came out with Thoreau's *A Week on the Concord and Merrimack Rivers*, paid for at the author's expense. The book sold poorly, and 706 of the 1,000 copies were returned to the publisher. With one flop to his credit, no one wanted to publish *Walden*, Thoreau's second book. It would be five years before he would find a publisher for it. When it finally appeared in 1854, *Walden*, was not an instant success, but it sold slowly and steadily over a period of years.

Thoreau was not heartened by these experiences, and like Emily Dickinson, another Massachusetts author who prized her freedom and solitude, he withdrew from the world of professional writing. While he continued to write his journal and gave an occasional lecture, Thoreau would now earn his living from the family business and part-time surveying.

He continued to tramp through the woods on his long walks, making memorable trips to Canada, Cape Cod and the Maine woods. He especially loved Maine, and on his second trip there in 1853, a traveling companion hunted and killed a moose. Thoreau's reaction to the killing speaks volumes about his concern not just for helpless animals, but for the environment in general: ". . . how base . . . are the motives which commonly carry men into the wilderness," he wrote, ". . . they have no more love for wild nature than wood-sawyers have for forests . . . For one that comes with a pencil to sketch or sing, a thousand come with an axe or rifle."

Thoreau also believed fervently in conserving nature within the limits of towns and cities. "Each town should have a park, or rather a primitive forest, of five hundred or a thousand acres," he wrote, ". . . a common possession forever." Years before the first national park or forest was established, he called for "nature preserves . . . for inspiration and our own true recreation!" One of our first naturalists, Thoreau was also our first conservationist.

But the very same natural world that gave life to Thoreau was robbing him of it. Always careless about his health, he developed tuberculosis from overexposure to the elements and too many nights of sleeping outdoors in all kinds of weather. This, combined with the deadly graphite dust he breathed constantly in the pencil factory, shortened his life by decades.

By the spring of 1862, it was clear Thoreau was dying. He welcomed death without bitterness, accepting it as just another part of nature's cycle. He had many visitors, among them his old jailer and friend, Sam Staples. After visiting Thoreau, Staples told Emerson he "never saw a man die with so much pleasure and peace." The end came on May 6, 1862.

Among the many eulogies and tributes to the 45-year-old writer was a brief poem by Bronson Alcott's daughter, Louisa, who would later gain fame as the author of *Little Women*:

Spring comes to us in guise forlorn;
The bluebird chants a requiem;
The wallow-blossom wait for him;—
The Genius of the wood is gone.

Gone, perhaps, but not forgotten. *Walden* continues to challenge readers the world over. Thoreau's message that "the majority of men lead lives of quiet desperation" is more true today than it was in his own time. Thoreau's answer for the ills of modern times was to simplify life and find success not in the material things of the world but in the mind and spirit. Pursuing these goals leads us not only to an understanding of life, he believed, but of the universe itself. As Thoreau writes in *Walden*:

> *If the day and the night are such that you greet them with joy, and life emits a fragrance like flowers and sweet-scented herbs, is more elastic, more starry, more immortal—that is your success. All nature is your congratulation, and you have cause momentarily to bless yourself. The greatest gains and values are farthest from being appreciated. We easily come to doubt if they exist. We soon forget them. They are the highest reality. Perhaps the facts most astounding and most real are never communicated by man to man. The true harvest of my daily life is somewhat as intangible and indescribable as the tints of morning or evening. It is a little stardust caught, a segment of the rainbow which I have clutched.*

Chronology

━━━━━━━━━━━

July 12, 1817 born in Concord, Massachusetts

1837 graduates from Harvard University and returns to Concord

1843 travels to New York City, where he tutors Ralph Waldo Emerson's nephew

1845–47 lives in cabin at Walden Pond

1849 first book, *A Week on the Concord and Merrimack Rivers*, published; essay "Civil Disobedience" first appears

1854 *Walden* published

1857 visits Maine woods for third and last time

1859 father dies, takes over management of family pencil factory

1861 travels to Minnesota, his furthest trip west

May 6, 1862 dies of severe "bronchitis" in Concord

Further Reading

Thoreau's Works

Henry David Thoreau: A Man For Our Time (New York: Viking, 1967). Brief selections from *Walden* and other works, well chosen and beautifully illustrated by celebrated children's author and artist James Daugherty.

A Thoreau Trilogy (New York: W.W. Norton, 1951). A three-volume set of *Cape Cod, The Maine Woods* and *Walden*, well illustrated by Henry Bugbee Kane.

Walden (New York: Dodd, Mead, 1946). This large-print edition of Thoreau's classic work is unique for its many photographs of Walden Pond and the surrounding countryside Thoreau knew and loved.

Books About Henry David Thoreau

Robert Burleigh, *A Man Named Thoreau* (New York: Atheneum, 1985). A well-written juvenile biography, nicely illustrated by Lloyd Bloom.

Sterling North, *Thoreau of Walden Pond* (Boston: Houghton Mifflin, 1959). A good biography for young adults.

Richard Rulard, *Walden: A Collection of Critical Essays* (Englewood Cliffs, N.J.: Prentice-Hall, 1968). Another entry in the excellent series of Twentieth Century Interpretations.

Philip Van Doren Stern, *Henry David Thoreau: Writer and Rebel* (New York: Thomas Crowell, 1972). Excellent, more detailed biography of the author.

Walt Whitman:
The Poet Plus

Walt Whitman is shown here at his house on Mickle Avenue in Camden, New Jersey. In his last years, the poet finally achieved the honor and respect due to him, if not the financial rewards.
(Library of Congress)

In 1855, a book of poetry appeared that scandalized many Americans, bewildered others and delighted some. One of the delighted readers was a 46-year-old lawyer in Springfield, Illinois. The lawyer's partner had left a copy of the book in their office, and he casually picked it up and started reading. He liked what he read and began reading one of the poems aloud to his partner and a law student. There was something in the freshness and honesty of the poetry that appealed to the tall, lanky lawyer. It captured the spirit of America like nothing else he had read. It didn't even bother him that the poems were untitled and no two lines of verse rhymed.

———

The poet was Walt Whitman. The poetry-loving lawyer was Abraham Lincoln. In five years, he would become the 16th president of the United States. Although Lincoln didn't know it, Whitman's life and his own would become inextricably linked.

At birth, Lincoln and Whitman would seem to have had little in common. Lincoln was born in a log cabin in 1809 and raised on the western frontier. Whitman was born on Long Island, New York, ten years later on May 31, and grew up in Brooklyn, already a small, thriving city next to New York City. However, both men's fathers were carpenters, and both had little formal education.

While Whitman did not become a lawyer, his first job, at age 13, was running errands in a law office. The young lawyers in the firm took a personal interest in this big, strapping boy who had already dropped out of school. They encouraged him to read, helped him with his writing and introduced him to the public library.

The young Whitman fell in love with books and read everything he could get his hands on. Attracted to writing, he landed a job setting type in a printing office. At 17, he turned to teaching, being no older than some of his students. Like Thoreau, he was a most unconventional schoolmaster. He, too, hated physical discipline, and often put aside the textbooks to talk with his students and teach from his own experiences. But teaching didn't satisfy the wanderlust that Whitman was beginning to feel—a love of rambling that would continue throughout his life.

At 19, he decided to publish his own newspaper. He bought some presses and set himself up as publisher, editor, chief reporter and delivery boy of *The Long Islander*. The newspaper lasted only two years, but Whitman would remain a working journalist for much of his life.

As magazines had become popular with the middle class in the first half of the 19th century, so newspapers became the daily reading material of the masses, particularly in the cities. It seems fitting that Walt Whitman should have become a part of this most democratic of literary movements, for he loved the common people every bit as much as Lincoln did.

This love for people was only rivaled by his love for the city so many of them lived in. Whitman loved New York with the same fervor that Thoreau felt for his woods. If Thoreau was on intimate terms with every tree and bird in Concord, Whitman knew every gas lamp on Broadway. His greatest thrill was riding down that famous boulevard in a horse-drawn omnibus, seated behind the driver. He knew every driver by name and even drove an omnibus himself several months for a sick friend. City life was a never-ending adventure for Whitman, a continual feast of sights, sounds and smells.

He was so busy enjoying life that Whitman didn't seem to have much time or energy left over to pursue a career. He bounced around Brooklyn and New York like a rubber ball, working part time as a journalist, going to the theater, dabbling in politics (he was a committed Democrat) and just loafing. This easygoing life-style continued well into his thirties. As his more down-to-earth brother George tersely put it, "We were all at work—all except Walt."

From his early twenties, Whitman dreamed of writing some "wonderful and ponderous book" that would capture the essence of the city, the people and America itself. Aside from his newspaper writing, however, Whitman's first literary efforts were anything but wonderful. His published stories, while socially conscious, were heavy-handed and moralistic. A novel, *Franklin Evans*, was a ponderous lesson on the evils of drinking. Whitman wisely realized that fiction was not his strength. Poetry, with its lyrical qualities and emotional pull, was better suited to his personality. In poems, he felt, he could express the inexpressible feelings and thoughts tumbling around inside his head.

By the middle of the 19th century, American poetry was flourishing. The country's most popular poet was Henry Wadsworth Longfellow. A scholar and literary man, Longfellow established an American tradition in poetry, just as Irving and Cooper did in prose. His famous long narrative poems, such as *Hiawatha* and *The Courtship of Miles Standish*, celebrated American history and folklore. Like his fellow poets James Russell Lowell and John Greenleaf Whittier, Longfellow was a romantic and a sentimentalist. Their poetry was bound by the strict conventions of meter and rhyme that had been developed in Europe hundreds of years before. This poetry had little to do with the robust rhythms of contemporary American life.

Whitman quickly decided that what he had to say in his poems couldn't be neatly packaged in such dainty verse. Pleasant rhymes and standard poetic forms had no place in his free-wheeling universe. As Adrien Soutenburg and Laura Nelson Baker point out in their excellent biography, Whitman sought a poetic form that was "oceanic, with verse that recalled the waves, rising and falling, often sunny, now and then wild with storm, scarcely two alike in length or measure."

His subject would not be old stories or legends but the America he lived in. His central theme would not be romantic love but the love he felt for every living thing. Whitman's poetry wouldn't praise Grecian urns or lofty ideals but the most common, everyday things we all take for granted, such as the grass under our feet. Like the Transcendentalists, he saw the individual as the measure of all things. In his mystic philosophy, every human being was directly linked to every other human being, as well as every thing on earth, alive or inanimate. The bold opening lines of his first poem, "Song of Myself," was a battle cry for this philosophy and a whole new kind of poetry:

I celebrate myself, and sing myself,
And what I assume you shall assume,
For every atom belonging to me as good belongs to you.
I loaf and invite my soul,
I lean and loaf at my ease observing a spear of summer grass,
My tongue, every atom of my blood, formed from this soil,
this air,
Born here of parents born here from parents the same, and
their parents the same,
I, now thirty-seven years old in perfect health begin,
Hoping to cease not till death.

When Whitman completed 12 long poems, 80 pages in length, he called them collectively *Leaves of Grass* and started hunting for a publisher. No one would touch such a strange and outlandish work. Finally, Whitman went to a friend who ran a printing shop and paid to have it published himself. He went one better than the great writers before him and set the type himself.

In the first half of the 1850s, four great books burst onto the American literary scene—*The Scarlet Letter, Moby-Dick, Walden* and *Leaves of Grass. The Scarlet Letter* was immediately hailed as a masterpiece. *Walden* and *Moby- Dick* were largely ignored. But *Leaves of Grass* received a truly scathing reception. While some reviewers were thoughtfully appreciative of Whitman's poetry, others detested it. The critic in the *Criterion* called the book a "gathering of muck." The *Boston Intelligencer* labeled it "a mass of bombast, egotism, vulgarity and nonsense," and urged that the author be kicked "from all decent society." Whittier is said to have tossed his review copy from the poet into the fire. Even Walt's family found his poetry incomprehensible. Brother George "didn't think it worth reading."

But Whitman found one champion for his work in Ralph Waldo Emerson. The leading Transcendentalist and essayist, himself a poet, opened a glowing letter to Whitman with the words, "I greet you at the beginning of a great career . . ." Whitman was so taken with this praise that he had these glowing words printed in gold leaf on the spine of a second edition of *Leaves of Grass* the following year. Emerson was irked that Whitman hadn't asked his permission, and his warmth for the poet cooled considerably in years to come.

While other writers write one book and then move on to another, Whitman saw *Leaves of Grass* as the major work of his life. For the next 35 years he continued to tinker with it—adding new poems, revising old ones, rearranging others, always seeking perfection in his art. Like a fertile field of grass, the book would grow from 12 poems to some 400 by the time of Whitman's death. Despite continuing negative reviews and public neglect, Walt, the eternal optimist, hoped each new edition of his book would bring him fame and fortune. It never did.

But on the horizon, a national catastrophe was brewing that would even more severely test Whitman's spirits. In December 1860, South Carolina became the first state to secede from the Union over the question of slavery. It was soon followed by six other Southern states. Together, in early 1861, they established their own nation, the Confederate States of America. On April 12, Confederate troops fired on the federal garrison at Fort Sumter in Charleston Harbor. The Civil War had begun.

This bloody conflict stirred Whitman as it did no other writer of his time. America, for Whitman, "the greatest poem," was suddenly torn in half, with brother fighting against brother. Walt's own brother George enlisted as a lieutenant-colonel in the 51st New York Volunteers. When George was reported missing in action, Walt left his newspaper job and went to Washington, D.C. He found George alive with only a slight wound on his cheek. But many of his fellow Union soldiers were not so fortunate. The hospitals were overflowing with critically injured men and just as many deathly ill from unsanitary conditions. Walt Whitman, who had called all men brothers in his poetry, now decided to put his beliefs into practice. He became a male nurse, and stayed on in the capital to provide comfort and assistance to tens of thousands of sick and wounded Union soldiers.

Although officially a wound dresser, Walt took his duties far more personally. He regularly visited the sick wards, bringing a kind word, newspapers and magazines, and even food to the patients. The young soldiers, looked forward to the visits of "the old man," as they affectionately called him. Whitman displayed the courage of a soldier at the battlefront by constantly visiting sick wards where he could easily have caught a contagious disease.

The toll, both physically and emotionally, on the poet was heavy. In a letter to his mother Walt wrote, ". . . one's heart groans sick of war, after all, when you see what it really is: every once in a while I feel so horrified and disgusted—it seems to me like a great slaughterhouse . . ."

What hopes Whitman had for an end to the slaughter focused on one man—President Abraham Lincoln. Whitman saw in Lincoln the embodiment of all that was best about America. Although the two men never formally met, they knew each other intimately—Lincoln through Whitman's poetry and Whitman through Lincoln's words and deeds. From the window of his rooming house in the capital, Walt often saw the president passing by on his way to his night's lodgings just north of the city. "I see very plainly ABRAHAM LINCOLN'S dark brown face, with the deep-cut lines," wrote the poet. "the eyes, always to me with a deep latent sadness in the expression. We have got so that we exchange bows and very cordial ones."

Walt was at home in Brooklyn with his mother on April 15, 1865, when word came that Lincoln had died from an assassin's bullet only days after Confederate General Robert E. Lee had surrendered to Union General Ulysses Grant at Appomattox. "Mother prepared . . . meals . . . but not a mouthful was eaten all day by either of us . . ." he later recalled. "We got every newspaper morning and evening . . . and passed them silently to each other."

Watching the grim funeral procession a few days later in Washington, Whitman was inspired to write a lyrical elegy to the fallen leader, which was one of his finest poems—"When Lilacs Last In The Dooryard Bloomed." The poet wisely chose to express his grief and that of the nation indirectly, contrasting the beauty of nature

*This ornate frontispiece from an early
edition of "When Lilacs Last in the
Dooryard Bloomed" captures some of
the mysticism and poignancy of
Whitman's elegy. The coffin being
carried by the procession of mourners
contains the body of assassinated
president Abraham Lincoln.*
(Library of Congress)

in springtime, represented by the lilacs, with the tragedy of
Lincoln's death. In this memorable passage, Lincoln is symbolized
by a falling star in the heavens:

> *O western orb sailing the heaven,*
> *Now I know what you must have meant as a month since I*
> *walked,*
> *As I walked in silence the transparent shadowy night,*
> *As I saw you had something to tell as you bent to me night*
> *after night,*

*As you drooped from the sky low down as if to my side (while
the other stars all looked on),
As we wandered together the solemn night (for something I
know not what kept me from sleep),
As the night advanced, and I saw on the rim of the west how
full you were of woe,
As I stood on the rising ground in the breeze in the cool trans-
parent night,
As I watched where you passed and was lost in the netherward
black of the night,
As my soul in its trouble dissatisfied sank, as where
you sad orb,
Concluded, dropped in the night, and was gone.*

The war was over, but for Whitman it was not forgotten. In 1865, he published in pamphlet form a new collection of poems, *Drum-Taps*, about the war and his experience among the wounded and dying. The book received no better reception than *Leaves of Grass*, although one its poems, "O Captain! My Captain!," which also dealt with Lincoln's death, went on to become his most popular poem. Interestingly enough, the poem is filled with rhyme and conventional meter, and could have been written by Longfellow himself.

Walt was now gainfully employed as a clerk in the Department of the Interior in Washington. Six months after he started, the new secretary of the Interior accidentally came upon a copy of *Leaves of Grass* and was so shocked by it that he demanded Whitman be fired at once. Fortunately, his poetry was found to be less scandalous by the attorney general, who quickly hired Whitman to work in his department.

Postwar America, with its political corruption and greedy materialism, further checked Whitman's optimism. In a book of prose, *Democratic Vistas*, his criticism of his country is as stinging and perceptive as Mark Twain's would be years later:

*Never was there, perhaps, more hollowness at heart than . . . here in
the United States . . . What penetrating eye does not everywhere see
through the mask? . . . We live in an atmosphere of hypocrisy
throughout . . . The great cities reek with respectable as much as non-
respectable robbery and scoundrelism.*

But if Whitman's bright candle was dimmed by a changing world, it was never extinguished. Even a crippling stroke at age

54 did not embitter him. A year later, he left Washington and moved to Camden, New Jersey, where he lived with his brother George and his wife. Here, he returned to newspaper writing, regained his strength and kept writing poetry.

The world was beginning to catch up with Whitman's genius. His poetry won widespread praise in England, while more and more American intellectuals were recognizing his originality, if not his greatness. When a seventh edition of *Leaves of Grass* was banned in Boston, it only helped sales elsewhere in the country.

In 1884, Whitman bought his first and only house on rundown Mickle Street in Camden, and shared it with a housekeeper and a menagerie of animals. It wasn't much to look at, but appearances had never mattered to him. Here the famous and the common people came to visit and pay their respects to the writer who, in his old age, was called by many "the good gray poet." He suffered a second stroke shortly after his 69th birthday and died a few years later on March 20, 1891. His friends, who thought him penniless, were surprised to learn he had bought and paid for an expensive tomb for himself. In death, Whitman hoped to be remembered more than in life.

He need not have worried. Today, Walt Whitman is considered one of the greatest poets of the 19th century, and the father of modern American poetry. Although non-rhyming free verse is as old as the Bible, Whitman recast it in his own image and style. Not only did he liberate poetry from old forms and conventions, but he opened up a world of subjects that poets had not addressed before. By wedding his poems with philosophy, religion and mysticism, he made poetry matter as it never had before. Whitman's focus on himself in his poems led to a whole school of autobiographical, or "confessional," poets in the 20th century, ranging from Robert Lowell to beat poet Allen Ginsberg.

Like any great writer, Whitman is not without his faults. The very excesses of personality that give his poetry energy and grandeur at times make it bloated, boring and overbearing. At other times, as in "O Captain! My Captain!", he could sink into the very sentimentality he so detested.

In his best poetry, however, his long, rambling lines seem to encompass the universe and everything in it. In his life and art, Whitman was always struggling to be more than just a poet. As one friend aptly put it, he was "a poet plus something else." That something else might have been life itself. John Burroughs, the naturalist and another close friend, perhaps put it best when he wrote, "I have no more doubt of his greatness than I have at the sun at noonday . . . he has form as a tree, a river, the clouds, a cataract, or flash of lightning . . . and this is all the form he aims at."

Chronology

May 31, 1819	born in West Hills, Long Island, New York
1832	takes first job as errand boy in law office
1838	publishes and edits his own newspaper, the *Long Islander*
1845	becomes editor of the *Brooklyn Eagle*
1848	begins work on *Leaves of Grass*
1855	first edition of *Leaves of Grass* published
1862	goes to Washington, D.C. to find wounded brother and stays to work as male nurse in Civil War hospitals
1865	becomes a clerk in the Department of the Interior; Lincoln assassinated
1871	fifth edition of *Leaves of Grass* appears, also prose work, *Democratic Vistas*.
1873	suffers first stroke, which leaves him partially paralyzed
1874	moves to Camden, New Jersey to live with brother George and wife
1882	seventh edition of *Leaves of Grass* banned in Boston
1884	buys house on Mickle Street in Camden
March 20, 1891	dies of pneumonia in Camden

Further Reading

Whitman's Works

Complete Poetry and Selected Prose (Boston: Houghton Mifflin, 1959). An indispensable volume that includes the original preface to the first edition of Leaves of Grass and the prose work Democratic Vistas.

Walt Whitman's America (New York: World Publishing, 1964). A more digestible introduction to the author for young readers, this volumes includes selections from Leaves of Grass, Democratic Vistas, Specimen Days and Portraits of Lincoln, selected and illustrated by James Daughtery.

Books About Walt Whitman

Adrien Stoutenburg and Laura Nelson Baker, Listen America: A Life of Walt Whitman (New York: Charles Scribner's, 1968). An excellent young-adult biography of Whitman, the man and poet.

Paul Zweig, Walt Whitman: the making of the poet (New York: Basic Books, 1984). Recommended for older readers, this biography emphasizes the poet's early manhood through the Civil War years.

Emily Dickinson: Lady of Mystery, Poet of Greatness

This silhouette, made when Emily Dickinson was 15, is one of only two likenesses of the poet that exist. The other is a photograph taken when she was a young woman.
(Amherst College)

*L*avinia Dickinson was nearly through with her unhappy task. She had spent hours going through her dead sister's clothes and other belongings in her modest room in the family home. Then quite by accident, she made a startling discovery. In a locked box inside a drawer in a cherrywood bureau, she found packets of neatly rolled notepaper, each sheet carefully sewn together. On the notepaper were written poems in her late sister's handwriting. Lavinia knew her sister wrote verse throughout her life for her own amusement, but here were more than a thousand poems!

Although the two sisters had lived in the same house all their lives, it suddenly occurred to Lavinia that there was a side of her dead sister that she had hardly known. This side would soon be revealed to the world through that boxful of poems. The secret of the most secretive writer in American literature would finally be out. Only after her death would Emily Dickinson be recognized as one of the greatest poets America has produced.

Emily Elizabeth Dickinson was born in Amherst, Massachusetts, 100 miles west of Boston, on December 10, 1830. She was the second of three children. Her father, Edward Dickinson, was one of Amherst's leading citizens. He was a lawyer, treasurer of Amherst College and later a U.S. congressman. The Dickinsons lived in a large, square brick mansion built by Emily's grandfather. The house had three gates and was majestically guarded by a hemlock hedge and tall trees. It was the grandest house in town.

Emily, for all her shyness as an adult, was a lively, curious child with a sharp and witty mind. She was thin and somewhat plain, but her hair was a gorgeous reddish brown and her large brown eyes took in everything around her.

Amherst, despite being a college town, was no Concord. Intellectual curiosity was curbed by propriety and strong fundamentalist religious beliefs. As a child, Emily rebelled against her stern upbringing. Once, to avoid going to church and sitting through a long, tedious sermon, she hid in the cellar.

Edward Dickinson was not disappointed in her, however. He saw promise in his eldest daughter and, when she turned 16, sent her off to the Mount Holyoke Seminary for Women in nearby South Hadley. Emily didn't like the discipline at Mount Holyoke and resented her teachers' efforts to make her conform to their strict religious beliefs. She left after only one year and returned to Amherst. She would never leave home again, except for a trip to Washington, D.C., when she was 24, and two trips to Boston to consult with doctors about an eye problem.

Back home among the family she loved, Emily began her true education. She started reading and writing poetry. She was supremely self-critical, and her first efforts did not please her. She was encouraged to continue writing, however, by a young law student, Benjamin Newton, who worked in her father's office.

Like her sister, Lavinia, Emily would never marry. But five men would play important roles in her life and art. That Emily loved passionately and was deeply disappointed in love comes through clearly in her poems. Which of her five men was closest to her heart, and who may have broken it, remains a mystery to this day.

Benjamin Newton, who introduced Emily to Transcendental-ism, died from poor health in 1853. His death left a deep mark on her. No matter how humorous and delightful her future poems would be, the shadow of death and a tragic sense of life would never be far from her mind.

In July 1856, her older brother William married Susan Gilbert. Susan would become one of Emily's closest friends and confi-dants. She had a deep love of literature and would be one of the few people who would truly appreciate Emily's poems.

By now, Emily was writing seriously. She found her inspiration in the simplest things in life—the birds singing in the large trees outside her bedroom window, the simple household chores she performed daily, the shifting light of the ever-changing New England skies. Like Walt Whitman, Emily reacted against the sentimental, sugary poetry of her day. But unlike Whitman, her poems weren't self-conscious and self-promotional. Her voice was a quiet voice, full of humility but also of great wisdom and wit. It spoke simply and directly to the reader like an intimate friend, in colloquial, everyday language that was deceptively simple:

I'm nobody. Who are you?
Are you nobody too?
Then there's a pair of us.
Don't tell—they'd banish us, you know.

How dreary to be somebody
How public—like a frog—
To tell your name the livelong June
To an admiring bog.

The perfect Yankee housekeeper, Dickinson wasted no words, but went straight to the heart of her message. The form of this poem—brief quatrains, or four-lined stanzas, with some rhym-ing—is the form of nearly all her poems. She modeled it after the New England church hymns she had learned as a child and had come to love. Most of her poems are brief; all are untitled.

But however brief, Dickinson's poems are capable of summing up a universe. Here, she describes the movements of a bird seen in her yard with the kind of sharp eye that would make a naturalist like Thoreau envious:

A bird came down the walk:
He did not know I saw;

He bit an angleworm in halves
And ate the fellow raw.

And then he drank a dew
From a convenient grass,
And then hopped sidewise to the wall
To let a beetle pass.

He glanced with rapid eyes
That hurried all around;
They looked like frightened beads, I thought;
He stirred his velvet head

Like one in danger; cautious,
I offered him a crumb,
And he unrolled his feathers
And rowed him softer home

Than oars divide the ocean,
Too silver for a seam,
Or butterflies, off banks of noon,
Leap, plashless, as they swim.

The power of observation that misses not the tiniest detail, the keen sense of humor, the stunning imagery and the sense of eternity that ends the poem are all characteristic of Dickinson's best work. She was always finding life's eternal meaning in the simplest things. Or as Van Wyck Brooks puts it, "She domesticated the universe and read her own experience into the motions of nature and the world she observed."

Emily's sister-in-law Sue recognized her talent, if not yet her genius. She arranged a meeting between the shy poet and Samuel Bowles, editor of the *Springfield Republican*, the most prestigious newspaper in the region. Bowles was charmed by Dickinson and delighted with her poetry. But when he published two of her poems in his paper in May 1861, one of them was heavily edited. Emily was furious and regretted ever letting her work see the public light. She still held Bowles in high regard, however, and may even have fallen in love with him.

Bowles had a rival for Emily's affections. He was Reverend Charles Wadsworth of Philadelphia, a spellbinding Presbyterian minister who Emily heard by chance on a return trip from Washington in 1855. Wadsworth, unfortunately, was a married man, and any romance between the two was doomed from the start. He visited her once in Amherst and later moved to California.

But a third man of the world was about to enter Emily's life and to have a profound effect on her career as a writer. In April 1862, Emily read an article in the *Atlantic Monthly* magazine, written by the critic Thomas Wentworth Higginson. Higginson urged young American writers to "charge your style with life . . ." Emily was inspired by the article and wrote to its author, including four of her poems with her letter. Here, perhaps, was the master she had sought who would help to guide her in her writing.

Higginson was a kind, thoughtful man, but he lacked great literary gifts or the ability to recognize them in others. He called Emily's thoughts and words "beautiful," but was perplexed by her poetry. He tried to get her to fit her poems into a more conventional mode, with flowing lines and regular rhyme schemes. He

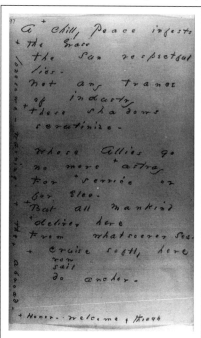

Dickinson revised each of her poems
many times until she was satisfied
with it. Then she would copy the
poem onto notepaper carefully
stitched together on a long roll. Note
the writing in the margin.
(Amherst College Library)

was totally oblivious to the originality and genius of her work. Fearing, perhaps rightly, that her verse would be rejected by the public and critics alike, Higginson discouraged her from attempting to get it published as it was. Emily saw no way she could change her writing style and, based on Higginson's advice, decided it was best to keep her writing to herself and a few friends. Thus, a great literary career may have been aborted due to the misguided "help" of one man!

But the poems continued to come. She would jot down ideas as they came to her, on the back of an envelope or a piece of scrap paper, while cooking a meal or cleaning the house. Later she would develop the idea into a poem, sitting in her upstairs corner bedroom by a Franklin stove. Sometimes she would revise one poem a dozen or more times before she was satisfied with it. In 1862 alone, she turned out an astonishing 365 poems.

What did poetry mean to Emily Dickinson? Here is how she described it to Higginson in a letter: "If I read a book and it makes my whole body so cold no fire ever can warm me, I know *that* is poetry. If I feel physically as if the top of my head were taken off, I know *that* is poetry. These are the only ways I know it. Is there any other way?"

Susan continued to encourage Emily to submit her poems for publication, but with little success. A few times she managed to submit them without her sister-in- law's knowledge. When Emily found out, she was furious. But there was another person who met with greater success in convincing Emily she should share her poems with the world.

Helen Hunt Jackson had grown up in Amherst and had even played with Emily when they were small children. By the 1870s, Jackson had become one of the most popular authors of her day, chiefly for her romantic novel, *Ramona*. Unlike her friend Higginson, Jackson saw that Emily was a poet of real stature. Jackson was asked to contribute to an anthology of poetry by important American poets and pleaded with Dickinson to submit something of her own for the collection. Emily was flattered but also fearful of seeing her work "revised" again by other hands. After Jackson had secretly submitted one of her poems, Emily reluctantly gave in. The 20-year-old poem, unsigned like all the others, was mistakenly attributed by many readers to Ralph Waldo Emerson. It remains one of her best-known poems:

Emily Dickinson

Success is counted sweetest
By those who ne'er succeed,
To comprehend a nectar
Requires sorest need.

Not one of all the purple host*
Who took the flag today
Can tell the definition
So clear of victory

As he defeated, dying,
On whose forbidden ear
The distant strains of triumph
Burst agonized and clear.

* army

Emily's worst fears were realized. The editors made five changes in the 12-line poem. It was the last time a poem of hers would appear in print in her lifetime.

By the mid-1870s, Emily had practically stopped writing poetry. She poured out her feelings and thoughts in letters to a few close friends. Her unhappiness over failed romances, her frail health and the death of her father in 1874 all contributed to the lessening of her creative drive and her deepening seclusion from the world. Now in her forties, she hardly left the big brick house and would often stay upstairs when guests came to call—even personal friends such as Samuel Bowles.

But Dickinson was not quite the "Queen Recluse" she now called herself. She loved children and often baked cookies for those in her neighborhood. Tramps, gypsies and Indian women who came looking for a handout or brought something to sell always found her generous, warm and easy to talk with.

Then one more opportunity for personal happiness unexpectedly arose. An old friend of Emily's father, Judge Otis Lord of Salem, lost his wife. Despite the 21-year difference in their ages, Lord wooed Emily, and she accepted his affections. However, when he proposed marriage, she turned him down to nurse her sick mother. Judge Lord died in 1884, and soon after Emily suffered a serious kidney disease. Bedridden and dying, she wrote her last note to the people who perhaps understood her best—the neighborhood children: "Little Cousins, called back—Emily." She went into a coma and died a few days later on May 15, 1886.

Emily had asked her sister to burn her poems and papers, but when Lavinia discovered the treasure trove of poems, she was unable to carry out the request. Instead, she turned to Higginson to help her find a publisher for Emily's poems. He was no more enthusiastic about her poetry than when Emily was alive, but agreed to prepare a collection for a book. *Poems by Emily Dickinson* appeared in 1890 and included 114 poems. Surprisingly, the public loved her poetry, despite heavy-handed editing, while the critics of the day still rejected them. Two more volumes of poems and two volumes of her letters followed within the next six years. Emily's niece, Martha Dickinson Bianchi, published three more collections of her aunt's poetry between 1914 and 1932. But it wasn't until the 1950s that a definitive, unedited edition of the complete poems revealed the full genius of Emily Dickinson.

Today, the "Queen Recluse" is the beloved poet of millions. Whatever price she paid in life for her withdrawal from society was reimbursed handsomely in the depth and richness of her poetry. Perhaps, only by isolating herself from the world could she write so subjectively about it. Because she lived apart, her writing is universal and seems to stand outside of human history, but never outside the human heart.

Of all the great 19th-century American writers, Emily Dickinson remains the most timeless and the most personal. She escaped the sense of original sin that haunted Hawthorne and Melville and expressed none of the national spirit that permeates Cooper and Whitman. Yet, through the tiny window of her soul, she saw the full scope of human existence in all its light and shadows. For Emily Dickinson, poetry was her way of communicating with the larger world she shied away from. Perhaps all her work could be best summed up in these tender and moving lines:

This is my letter to the world
That never wrote to me,
The simple news that nature told
With tender majesty.

Her message is committed
To hands I cannot see.
For love of her, sweet countrymen,
Judge tenderly of me.

Chronology

December 10, 1830	born in Amherst, Massachusetts
1846	attends Mount Holyoke Female Seminary in South Hadley
1853	Benjamin Newton, first friend and mentor, dies
1855	travels to Washington, D.C. with sister to visit father, then serving in Congress
1858	begins writing poetry seriously
1861	two poems published in the *Springfield Republican*
1862	starts friendship and correspondence with critic Thomas Wentworth Higginson
1874	father dies
1878	agrees to have one poem appear in prestigious anthology under urging of friend Helen Hunt Jackson
May 15, 1886	dies at home of Bright's disease
1890	*Poems by Emily Dickinson* appears posthumously

Further Reading

Dickinson's Works
The Complete Poems of Emily Dickinson (Boston: Little, Brown, 1960). All the poetry with a useful first-line index, edited by Thomas H. Johnson.

Poems of Emily Dickinson (New York: Thomas Crowell, 1964). A good cross-section of her poetry, interestingly categorized and selected by Helen Plotz.

Books About Emily Dickinson
Edna Barth, *I'm Nobody! Who Are You? The Story of Emily Dickinson* (New York: Seabury Press, 1971). A strong young-adult biography, including a good selection of her most famous poems.

Aileen Fisher and Olive Rabe, *We Dickinsons* (New York: Atheneum, 1965). The life of the poet as seen through the eyes of her brother Austin. An intriguing departure from the standard biography.

Jean Gould, *Miss Emily* (Boston: Houghton Mifflin, 1946). A rather old-fashioned, fictionalized biography for young readers.

Polly Longsworth, *Emily Dickinson: Her Letter to the World* (New York: Thomas Crowell, 1965). A solid biography that uses the poetry and letters, to illustrate the writer's life.

William Luce, *The Belle of Amherst* (Boston: Houghton Mifflin, 1976). A fascinating one-woman play in which Dickinson talks about her life and work.

Mark Twain:
The People's Author

This photograph was taken in the author's last years when he referred to himself as "the most conspicuous person on the planet." Considering his fame and the popularity of his books, this is probably not a great exaggeration.
(Library of Congress)

*N*o American writer of the 19th century was as beloved and celebrated as Mark Twain. Twain's career embodied all the complexities and contradictions of the America of his age. He despised his country's growing greed for money and power, and yet he spent much of his adult life amassing wealth. He was a writer of wisdom, wit and sound judgment, but in business matters he could be gullible and foolish. He was America's greatest humorist, yet he ended up mankind's darkest cynic and most savage critic.

Mark Twain realized the American Dream of success that eluded other great writers from Poe to Whitman, only to find it empty and valueless.

———

   Twain, whose real name was Samuel Longhorne Clemens, was born on November 30, 1835, in Florida, Missouri. Halley's comet burned brightly in the sky the night of his birth, an omen of good things to come for this sickly, premature baby.
   Clemens's father, John, was a failure as both a lawyer and a storekeeper. A move to nearby Hannibal did little to improve his fortunes. He died a broken man at 49, when Sam was 12. Life in Hannibal for the growing boy was both bleak and full of promise. The Mississippi River flowed through the sleepy town, and its great riverboats, like exotic caravans, fired young Sam's imagination. "When I was a boy, there was but one permanent ambition among my comrades," he later wrote in his classic book, *Life on the Mississippi*, "That was to be a steamboatman."
   Clemens would realize that ambition, but not for many years. After his father's death, he went to work as a printer to help support the family. He first worked for his older brother Orion, who ran a newspaper in Hannibal, and then moved East where he toiled for four years in several cities as a traveling typesetter.
   Turning 21, Clemens decided there had to be an easier way to make a living. America was bursting with opportunities. Gold and silver had been discovered in the Far West. Land was cheap. Young men were leaving home to explore the world and get rich quick. Clemens had heard about the fabulous coca trade in the Amazon River region of Brazil. He boarded a riverboat in Cincinnati, Ohio and headed south. But he fell in love all over again with the Mississippi and asked the boat's pilot to take him on as an apprentice or "cub." The young man learned every twist and turn of the mighty river from St. Louis to New Orleans. In two years he earned his license as a steamboat pilot and also found a new name. The boatmen's cry for a depth of two fathoms, or 12 feet, was "Mark Twain!" Sam Clemens liked the sound of that and would remember it later when he became a writer.
   Clemens might have remained a contented riverboat pilot for years if the Civil War hadn't come along. The Mississippi was closed to commercial trade, and he suddenly found himself out of a job. Although Missouri remained in the Union, many Missouri-

ans were sympathetic to the Southern cause. Young Clemens was for a while one of these sympathizers, and had a brief and unspectacular career as a Confederate militiaman. He later wrote that he learned more about retreating "than the man that invented retreating."

Meanwhile, his brother Orion firmly supported the North, and was rewarded for his efforts by Lincoln's Republican administration. He was appointed secretary of the newly formed Nevada Territory. In July 1861, Orion left by stagecoach for Nevada, accompanied by Sam, who went along as his private secretary. Silver had been discovered in the Nevada hills, and Sam soon left his brother to join the stream of prospectors hoping to strike it rich. He didn't. Disappointed and broke, Sam wrote to Orion, "The fact is, I must have something to do, and that *shortly*, too, even writing."

He had dabbled in writing since he was 16 and had a sketch published in a Boston magazine. Now he turned to journalism for a living and was hired as a reporter by a newspaper in Virginia City for $25 a week. Clemens was no ordinary journalist. His specialty was writing humorous pieces and perpetrating hoaxes that poked fun at local citizens. On February 3, 1863, for the first time, he signed a published letter not Sam Clemens but "Yours, dreamily, Mark Twain."

When he went too far with one hoax, Twain was forced to leave town and headed to California, where he eventually tried mining again. In a saloon in a mining camp in Calaveras County, he heard a miner tell a tale about a jumping frog contest that he found very funny. He wrote his own version of the story and sent it East, where it was published in the New York *Saturday Press*. Eastern readers found Twain's tall tale hilarious. It was the start of the greatest success story in 19th-century American literature.

"The Celebrated Jumping Frog of Calaveras County" has been called by Twain scholar Justin Kaplan, "the dazzling landmark of Mark Twain's early career and a model for some of the best of his later work—the oral, humorous, first-person story rendered in print . . ."

The story concerns a miner, Jim Smiley, who will bet on anything. He finds a prize-jumping frog he names Dan'l Webster and challenges a stranger to a frog- jumping contest. While Smiley is off finding a frog for his rival, the stranger devises a clever scheme:

. . . he got the frog out and prized his mouth open and took out a teaspoon and filled him full of quail-shot—filled him pretty near up to his chin—and set him on the floor. Smiley . . . he ketched a frog and fetched him in and give him to this feller, and says:
"'Now, if you're ready, set him alongside of Dan'l, with his forepaws just even with Dan'l's, and I'll give him the word,' Then he says, 'One-two-three-git!' and . . . the new frog hopped off lively, but Dan'l give a heave and hysted up his shoulders—so—like a Frenchman, but it warn't no use—he couldn't budge; he was planted as solid as a church, and he couldn't no more stir than if he was anchored out . . .
"The feller took the money and started away, and when he was going out at the door he sorter jerked his thumb over his shoulder—so—at Dan'l and says again, very deliberate, 'Well,' he says, 'I don't see no p'ints about that frog that's better'n any other frog.'

Twain's use of everyday American speech and local dialect was something new in American literature. All the great writers before him, from Irving to Melville, told their stories in formal, sometimes outdated, English. Cooper's Natty Bumppo talked more like an Upstate aristocrat than a rude backwoodsman. Twain captured the speech of the common American and infused new life into American writing. Through his folksy narrators, he could poke fun at society and institutions in a way that made readers both laugh and think. Twain was a humorist, but soon he would reveal a serious bent.

The notoriety of "The Jumping Frog" landed the young writer a plum newspaper assignment to the Hawaiian Islands, then known as the Sandwich Islands. Once there, he had another stroke of good fortune. Survivors of a clipper ship disaster reached the Islands and were immediately interviewed by Twain, who was paid $300 for his exclusive scoop. He returned to San Francisco, and in October 1866, gave his first public lecture, about life on the Sandwich Islands. His humorous delivery and folksy Missourian drawl made him a hit with audiences. It was the beginning of his 40-year career as a public speaker and entertainer.

In 1867, Twain took another voyage, this one across the Atlantic to Europe and the Holy Land. Unlike American authors before him, he found little to admire in Europe. With great gusto and wit, Twain poked fun at the pretensions of these older civilizations. Americans, more confident now of their own national character, loved his articles. They were collected into his first book, *The Innocents Abroad*, two years later. The book was a best-seller and set the style for a series of partly fictionalized, partly autobiographical travel books, including *Roughing It* (1872), *A Tramp Abroad* (1880) and *Following the Equator* (1897). The same middle-class readers who had made the reputations of Cooper, Hawthorne and the early Melville took Twain to their hearts and dubbed him "The People's Author."

In February 1870, Twain married Olivia Langdon, heiress of a wealthy New York family, whose brother he'd met on the ship to Europe. The young couple moved to Hartford, Connecticut the following year. Here, Twain designed a dream house that befitted America's most prosperous author. The house, which is today a museum, was partly built in the shape of a riverboat. Twain's neighbors were Harriet Beecher Stowe, author of *Uncle Tom's Cabin*, and editor and essayist Charles Dudley Warner. Warner collaborated with Twain on his first novel, *The Gilded Age*, in 1873. The book satirized American society's preoccupation with materialism so effectively that its title came to represent the era.

In Hartford, Twain began to write a string of books that would solidify his reputation—*Life on the Mississippi*, *The Prince and the Pauper* and *Tom Sawyer*. In this last book, aimed at the growing juvenile audience, Twain looked back fondly on his own boyhood and the great river that played so large a part in it. Hannibal became St. Petersburg in the novel, and Tom Sawyer and his friends were idealized versions of young Twain and the people he grew up with. The book became an instant classic of children's literature.

In 1876, Twain started work on a new book that was to be a kind of sequel to *Tom Sawyer*. "Began another boys' book," he wrote to his close friend, the critic and novelist William Dean Howells. ". . . I like it only tolerably well, as far as I have got, and may possibly pigeonhole it or burn the MS when it is done."

Fortunately, he didn't burn it, but continued to work on the troubled book, on and off, for seven years. What started out as "another boys' book" became something very different. Huck Finn, Tom Sawyer's pal and the novel's hero, was a more rebellious youth, who lived with an alcoholic father who regularly beat him. Huck's America was filled with corruption, murder and injustice, and was probably far closer to the reality of Twain's childhood than *Tom Sawyer*.

At the heart of *The Adventures of Huckleberry Finn* is the warm friendship between Huck and Jim, a runaway slave. Together they leave St. Petersburg on a raft and float down the Mississippi, having one adventure after another. Twain's use of American

*This frontispiece to the 1885 edition
of* Huckleberry Finn *was the work of
the celebrated illustrator E. W.
Kemble, who also illustrated other
Twain works.*
(Library of Congress)

Dialect reached its creative peak in *Huckleberry Finn*, which is told
in the first person by Huck himself.

In this excerpt, Huck, whose conscience bothers him about
aiding Jim, has just written a note to Jim's owner, Miss Watson,
revealing Jim's whereabouts:

*I felt good and all washed clean of sin for the first time I had ever felt
so in my life, and I knowed I could pray now. But I didn't do it straight
off but laid the paper down and set there thinking—thinking how good
it was all this happened so, and how near I come to being lost and
going to hell. And went on thinking. And got to thinking over our trip
down the river; and I see Jim before me all the time: in the day and
in the nighttime, sometimes moonlight, sometimes storms, and we
a- floating along, talking and singing and laughing. But somehow I*

couldn't seem to strike no places to harden me against him, but only the other kind. I'd see him standing my watch on top of his'n, 'stead of calling me, so I could go on sleeping; and see how glad he was when I come back out of the fog; . . . and at last I struck the time I saved him by telling the men we had smallpox aboard, and he was so grateful, and said I was the best friend old Jim ever had in the world and the only one he's got now; and then I happened to look around and see that paper.

It was a close place. I took it up, and held it in my hand. I was a-trembling, because I'd got to decide, forever, betwixt two things, and I knowed it. I studied a minute, sort of holding my breath, and then says to myself:

"All right, then I'll go to hell"—and tore it up.

It was awful thoughts and awful words but they was said. And I let them stay said; and never thought no more about reforming . . . And for a starter I would go to work and steal Jim out of slavery again; and if I could think up anything worse, I would do that, too; because as long as I was in and in for good, I might as well go the whole hog.

Twain's ironic reversal of "good" and "evil" in this brief passage was a more powerful condemnation of slavery than a hundred abolitionist pamphlets. Jim is eventually brought to "justice," but escapes again with Huck and Tom Sawyer's help. The book ends with Huck deciding to "light out for the Territory" rather than be adopted by Tom's Aunt Sally, who would "sivilize" him. After reading Twain's vivid depiction of the corrupt and immoral society around him, the reader can't help but feel Huck has made the right choice.

"It's the best book we've had," novelist Ernest Hemingway said of *Huckleberry Finn*. "All American writing comes from that." The critics in 1883 were not so generous. One called the book "coarse and dreary fun." No less an authority on children's literature than Louisa May Alcott, author of *Little Women*, wrote, "If Mr. Clemens cannot think of something better to tell our pure-minded lads and lasses, he had best stop writing for them." Many public libraries followed the lead of the Concord, Massachusetts Library Committee and removed the book from its shelves. Sad to say, *Huck Finn* is still banned in some school libraries in America today.

Huckleberry Finn is generally considered to be Twain's finest book, and its initial reception deeply troubled him. But he soon had greater troubles. Always looking for new inventions and schemes to increase his wealth. Twain began investing in an automatic typesetting machine in 1880. The machine, run by one operator, could do the work of four workers setting type by hand. The idea was sound, but the actual invention was poorly designed and doomed to failure. Over 15 years, Twain sank $200,000 into the machine, and it brought him close to financial ruin.

Some years later, when an inventor came to him offering stock in what he claimed would be a major breakthrough in mass communications, Twain was leery of getting involved in another quack invention. He later wrote, " . . . I didn't want it at any price . . . He said he would sell me as much as I wanted for $500 . . . But I . . . resisted all those temptations—resisted them easily . . ."

If Twain hadn't resisted, he would have earned back nearly all the money he'd lost on the typesetting machine. The inventor was Alexander Graham Bell, and his invention, the telephone. Interestingly enough, the author was later the first person to have a telephone installed in his home.

In 1891, Twain left his Hartford mansion forever and moved to Europe to live for nine years in self-exile. His financial disappointments and the public's rejection of his masterpiece darkened his vision of American society, and this was reflected in his writing.

A Connecticut Yankee in King Arthur's Court (1889) is, on the surface, an exciting time-travel adventure, in which a Hartford man is transported back to medieval England through a blow on the head. Between the lines, however, the book is a damning indictment of both the age of chivalry, which the author depicts as brutal and heartless, and the modern technological world, represented by the Yankee. By creating new weapons of destruction, "Sir Boss," as he is called, helps to win King Arthur a bloody victory on the battlefield.

Pudd'nhead Wilson (1894) is a detective mystery involving two children, one white the other mulatto, who are switched at birth. One is later exposed as a murderer on the evidence of fingerprints. The book, Twain's last major work, was his strongest statement against slavery since *Huckleberry Finn*.

After the national economic depression of 1893, Mark Twain found himself $100,000 in debt. He made a vow to pay back every penny and went off on an around-the-world lecture tour. The tour was a personal and financial success. Everywhere the 60-year-old author went he was treated like royalty. He was just regaining his spirits when news reached him that Susy, his favorite daughter, had died suddenly of meningitis at age 24. A few years later, in a letter to Howells, he wrote, referring to the year he moved to Hartford: "There was no Susy then—and there is no Susy now.

And how much lies between—one long lovely stretch of scented fields, and meadows, and shady woodlands; and suddenly Sahara!"

In the arid desert of his loss, Twain's imagination turned even darker, his outlook on life, bleak and cynical. In works he was afraid to publish, for fear of losing his public, he railed against war, political power and civilization itself. Some of these works were not printed until many years after his death, startling readers with an entirely different side of the "people's author."

The last decade of Twain's life was outwardly peaceful, as he basked in the acclaim of an international audience and once more acquired a modest fortune. He was hailed as "the most conspicuous person on the planet." It was said that a letter simply addressed "Mark Twain" would get to him. As 1910 approached and astronomers predicted the return of Halley's comet, Twain mused, "It will be the greatest disappointment of my life if I don't go out with Halley's comet." He did, dying on April 21 of that year.

Mark Twain remains a major figure in American literature, although for partly different reasons now than in his own lifetime. He has proved to be more than a humorist, a regional writer and a front-porch philosopher. He is perceived now as an artist of great depth, who, in his best books, looked at life in America unflinchingly, finding much to celebrate and much to criticize. As Van Wyck Brooks has written, he "was to make the Mississippi a focus of the national mind, as Washington Irving earlier had made the Hudson, on a scale incomparably larger and richer than Irving's."

Twain had seen more of America than any other writer of his century, and had captured the color, diversity and character of its people in his prose, much as Whitman had in his poetry. In his strengths and weaknesses as a man and writer, Twain symbolized the America of his time. Like the ambitious young nation, Twain's books were often poorly planned, meandering and at times even childish and petulant in their humor. Even his masterpiece, *Huckleberry Finn*, is uneven, its final chapters sinking to a level of low comedy that is out of keeping with the best parts of the book.

The tradition of American individualism that began with Washington Irving's American tales reached its culmination in the work of Mark Twain—who longed for the past, fretted about the present and feared for the future. The nation that was still a youth at his birth was a full-grown adult in the world of nations by the time of his passing. But even as Twain and the 19th century were coming to an end, a new generation of writers was writing about new problems and challenges in a radically changed America.

Chronology

November 30, 1835	born in Florida, Missouri
1839	family moves to Hannibal, on the Mississippi
1846–56	works as printer for brother Orion and for other newspapers in the East
1859	becomes licensed riverboat pilot on the Mississippi
1861	goes West to Nevada with Orion, prospects for silver and begins career as journalist
1865	"The Celebrated Jumping Frog of Calaveras County" appears
1866	gives first public lecture about the Sandwich (Hawaiian) Islands
1869	first book, *The Innocents Abroad*, published
1871	moves to Hartford, Connecticut with wife Olivia
1876	*Tom Sawyer* published
1884	*Huckleberry Finn* published
1889	*A Connecticut Yankee in King Arthur's Court* published
1893	financially ruined by national depression
1895	goes on around-the-world lecture tour to pay off debts
1900	returns to America after nine years abroad
April 21, 1910	dies in Connecticut

Further Reading

Twain's Works

The Adventures of Huckleberry Finn (Pleasantville, N.Y.: Reader's Digest, 1986). An excellent young-adult edition of Twain's finest work, with E. W. Kemble's memorable illustrations from the 1885 edition.

The Adventures of Tom Sawyer (Pleasantville, N.Y.: Reader's Digest, 1985). Another good young-adult edition, with illustrations by Paul Geiger.

The Complete Short Stories of Mark Twain (Garden City, N.Y.: Doubleday, 1957). Twain's total output of stories from "The Celebrated Jumping Frog" to "The Mysterious Stranger" are found here, with an introduction by Charles Neider.

A Connecticut Yankee in King Arthur's Court (New York: Harper & Row, 1917). An easy-to-read edition of Twain's exciting, if often dark, satire of the past and present.

The Portable Mark Twain selected and introduced by Bernard De Voto (New York: Viking, 1968). Includes the complete *Huckleberry Finn*, selections from numerous other works, such as the *Autobiography*, and Twain's letters.

Books About Mark Twain

Edwin Gordon, *Mark Twain* (New York: Crowell-Collier Press, 1966). A good introduction to the author's life that emphasizes his many careers.

Jim Hargrove, *Mark Twain: The Story of Samuel Clemens* (Chicago: Childrens Press, 1984). Informative biography that stresses the early years.

Sterling North, *Mark Twain and the River* (Boston: Houghton Mifflin, 1961). Excellent biography that deals only briefly with the mature author.

Robert Quackenbush, *Mark Twain? What Kind of Name Is That?: A Story of Samuel Leghorne Clemens* (Englewood Cliffs, N.J.:

Prentice-Hall, 1984). A humorous juvenile biography, illustrated by the author in cartoon style.

James Playsted Woods, *Spunkwater! Spunkwater!—A Life of Mark Twain* (New York: Pantheon Books, 1968). A more serious and balanced portrait of the writer's life.

Stephen Crane: Rebel Writer

Stephen Crane became famous at age 23 with the publication of The Red Badge of Courage. *A little of the intensity and restlessness that drove the writer to burn himself out at an early age is revealed in this photograph.*
(Library of Congress)

*F*rom Washington Irving onward, American writers had rarely described the world around them as it really was. They wrote in a romantic tradition that was several levels removed from "real life." The characters and events they depicted in their prose were full of mystery and adventure. They dealt in symbols, allegories and morals. Nathaniel Hawthorne actually called his books "romances," not novels.

By the century's last two decades, American writers could no longer ignore reality. The United States had been transformed from a nation of farmers and small towns into a manufacturing, industrial giant. Large cities had mushroomed into metropolises, and large towns into small cities. Tens of thousands of immigrants from Europe and elsewhere swarmed to America's shores in search of freedom and new opportunities. But as the country fulfilled its Manifest Destiny and became settled from coast to coast, many newcomers ended up in cities like New York and Chicago, where they worked in grim factories and lived in crowded slums.

This new urban America attracted the attention of young writers, who founded a new style of writing, called realism, to describe it. Realism was, in the words of William Dean Howells—its chief spokesman in America—"nothing more or less than the truthful treatment of material." Realistic writers looked at the world around them, not as it could or should be but as it really was. Of all the talented writers who wrote in this new, bold style before 1900, one stands out from all the others—Stephen Crane.

Stephen Crane's courage and spirit came naturally. His great-uncle and namesake was a hero in the American Revolution. Captured by Hessian soldiers, he refused to reveal the whereabouts of American troops and was summarily shot. Crane's father was a respected Methodist minister, who preached forgiveness for the South after the Civil War, when most Northerners only had hatred in their heart for the defeated enemy.

Crane was born in Newark, New Jersey on November 1, 1871, the youngest of 14 children. His father died when he was nine, and his strong-willed mother moved the family to Asbury Park, a resort community. Stephen attended preparatory school and then spent two semesters at college, the second one at Syracuse University in upstate New York.

College held little interest for young Crane. "Not that I dislike books, but the cut-and-dried curriculum . . . did not appeal to me," he later wrote. "Humanity was a more interesting study." The humanity he choose to study was the downtrodden, the poor and the hopeless. As a student, he haunted the night courts and slums of Syracuse, watching and listening to the people who lived their lives outside the law. Crane believed these people were not innately evil but often had no other way to make a living. He began to write short sketches and newspaper articles about them.

Crane's only other passion in school was baseball. He was a first-rate catcher and shortstop on the Syracuse team and even seriously considered becoming a professional player for a while.

Joining some friends in New York City, Crane lived in a ramshackle boardinghouse on the crowded city's East Side. His older brother Townley was an established journalist and helped Stephen to get free-lance writing assignments for several newspapers. Life in New York was a struggle for the young writer. He lived hand-to-mouth much of the time, relying on the generosity of friends and relatives when his funds ran out. He ate poorly and suffered from terrible coughs and severe indigestion. For pleasure, he would leave his modest room on East 23rd Street and head downtown to an even more squalid neighborhood—the Bowery. Here the dregs of society lived—men and women without any means of support who ate in soup kitchens and often slept in the streets. Crane listened and talked to them about their sad lives. Out of these experiences, and a brief encounter with a streetwalker he met in a Syracuse police court, he fashioned his first novel, *Maggie: A Girl of the Streets*.

Written when Crane was 20, *Maggie* struck the quiet literary landscape of America with the force of a bombshell. In sharp, realistic prose, it told the tragic story of a girl raised by two brutish parents in a New York slum. She goes to work in a collar factory, only to fall in love with a man who abandons her. Disowned by her hypocritical mother and brother, Maggie turns to prostitution and ends up killing herself. The book is totally honest, devoid of sentimentality and offers no moral. The author leaves it to the reader to be angered by the social conditions that destroy the young girl and perhaps do something to change them. It was the first truly realistic novel in American fiction, and it was rejected at first by every publisher the young author sent it to.

Finally, in 1892, Crane convinced a New York publisher of medical and religious books to publish it, paying them $869 he had borrowed from one of his brothers. Afraid his name would prejudice reviewers who had read his news stories, Crane used the pseudonym "Johnston Smith."

With review copies he sent to numerous critics and writers, Crane included this message: "It is inevitable that you will be greatly shocked by this book but continue please with all possible courage to the end. For it tries to show that environment is a tremendous thing in the world and frequently shapes life . . ."

One reader who was not shocked was writer Hamlin Garland. Garland, who was 11 years older than Crane, wrote realistic stories and novels about farmers in his native Wisconsin. He was impressed by the novel, reviewed it favorably and sent a copy to William Dean Howells, known as the "dean of American letters." Both Garland and Howells became strong supporters of Crane. Howells claimed in an interview that Crane ". . . . is very young, but he promises splendid things."

The public at the time, however, saw nothing splendid in *Maggie* and avoided it like the plague. Crane found himself using piles of unsold copies as chairs in his unfurnished one-room apartment.

He had no greater success as a newspaper writer. While *Maggie* was fiction written with objectivity, Crane's news stories were noteworthy for their subjectivity. He was too much of an artist to keep his personal feelings out of the events he reported. This tendency got him fired from more than one newspaper.

When Crane reported on a labor march in Asbury Park, he sharply contrasted the downtrodden marchers with the amused well-to-do resort people who watched them. Ironically, Crane's sympathetic but realistic description of the marchers was seen as an attack on the working man. The paper he wrote for, the conservative *New York Tribune*, was afraid of negative publicity and immediately fired Crane and his brother Townley. It was just the first of many misunderstandings that would plague the writer during his tempestuous career.

Frustrated by writing for the newspapers, Crane once more turned to fiction. While staying at a friend's, he chanced upon a series of magazine articles about the Civil War. The writing was bland and captured none of the human drama of the still well-remembered conflict. Crane recalled his brother Edmund's colorful descriptions of the Battle of Chancellorsville, Virginia, in which he had fought on the Union side. Crane decided to write his own war novel, drawing on Edmund's stories, articles and books he had read, and his own vivid imagination. He sat down and wrote at white heat for ten days and nights. The result was one of the most celebrated novels about war ever written—*The Red Badge of Courage*.

The "hero" of Crane's masterpiece was no great general or stalwart officer but an ordinary, young Union soldier named

The boredom of war is well captured in this picture of Union troops in the trenches before Petersburg, Virginia in June 1864. The Civil War battle described by Stephen Crane in The Red Badge of Courage *is believed to be the Battle of Chancellorsville, in which his brother Edmund participated.*
(National Archives)

Henry Fleming. Henry joins the Army in expectation of glory and fame on the battlefield. His illusions are quickly shattered when he first faces enemy fire and finds himself panicking along with the other soldiers around him:

> *. . . The youth turned his head, shaken from his trance by this movement as if the regiment was leaving him behind . . .*
> *He yelled then with fright and swung about. For a moment, in the great clamor, he was like a proverbial chicken. He lost the direction of safety. Destruction threatened him from all points.*
> *Directly he began to speed toward the rear in great leaps. His rifle and cap was gone. His unbuttoned coat bulged in the wind. The flap of his cartridge box bobbed wildly, and his canteen, by its slender cord, swung out behind. On his face was all the horror of those things which he imagined . . .*

Since he had turned his back upon the fight his fears had been wondrously magnified. Death about to thrust him between the shoulderblades was far more dreadful than death about to smite him between the eyes . . .

As he ran on he mingled with others. He dimly saw men on his right and on his left, and he heard footsteps behind him. He thought that all the regiment was fleeing, pursued by these ominous crashes.

Henry soon learns, however, that many of his comrades did not run away, but fought and died that day. He feels like a coward and envies the "red badge of courage" worn by the wounded. He returns to the regiment the next day and is caught up again in the fighting. He becomes a real hero, for the moment, and later leads a charge as flag-bearer:

The youth kept the bright colors to the front. He was waving his free arm in furious circles, the while shrieking mad calls and appeals, urging on those that did not need to be urged, for it seemed that the mob of blue men hurling themselves on the dangerous group of rifles were again grown suddenly wild with an enthusiasm of unselfishness.

He himself felt the daring spirit of a savage religion mad. He was capable of profound sacrifices, a tremendous death. He had no time for dissections, but he knew that he thought of the bullets only as things that could prevent him from reaching the place of his endeavor. There were subtle flashings of joy within him that thus should be his mind.

Henry Fleming emerges from the battlefield as a man, ready to leave the valley of death and live. This intensely personal view of modern warfare concentrates on the power of fear and man's struggle to conquer it. Crane's achievement is all the more stunning when one realizes he was born six years after the Civil War ended and never saw nor was in a battle. Yet his writing was so convincing that grizzled Civil War veterans wrote him, asking what regiment he had served in.

Prose was not the only avenue of expression for Stephen Crane. One night he heard William Dean Howells give a public reading of poems by Emily Dickinson. Crane felt inspired to write his own poetry, which proved to be unlike any other poems written up to that time. He didn't consider them poems at all; he called them "bitter little pills." More experimental than anything written by Dickinson or even Whitman, they are considered by many scholars as the predecessors of much modern poetry. These short, rhymeless verses are filled with symbolism and contain all the power and wisdom of biblical parables. Crane collected them into two volumes—*The Black Riders* and *War is Kind*. Neither work was understood or appreciated in his lifetime. Here is a typical poem, *The Wayfarer*:

> *The wayfarer*
> *Perceiving the pathway to truth,*
> *Was struck with astonishment.*
> *It was thickly grown with weeds.*
> *"Ha," he said,*
> *"I see that none has passed here*
> *In a long time."*
> *Later he saw that each weed*
> *Was a singular knife.*
> *"Well," he mumbled at last,*
> *"Doubtless there are other roads."*

While his poetry went largely unread, Crane's *Red Badge of Courage* was an instant success, both as a newspaper serial and later in book form. Critics on both sides of the Atlantic hailed the 24-year-old writer as a genius. But, unlike Mark Twain, fame and celebrity did not sit well with Stephen Crane. He had spent his life as an outsider, identifying with the outcasts of society, and did not feel comfortable in the role of an "establishment" writer. He also feared, rightly, that fame would turn him into a hack, writing merely for money and not artistic success. He fled New York City for Port Jervis, New York, where he continued to write, turning out stories and another novel in quick succession.

Crane shunned the many social invitations he received, but did accept one from the popular New York City Board of Police Commissioners president, Theodore Roosevelt. A few years later, the energetic and charismatic Roosevelt would become president of the United States. Crane told Roosevelt about the police corruption he had seen firsthand on the city streets, and the harassment of petty criminals, who were forced to pay for police "protection." Roosevelt promised to investigate the situation.

Soon after, Crane was a witness once more to an act of police brutality. Charles Becker, a notoriously corrupt policeman, assaulted a prostitute who had not paid him off. Crane testified against Becker in court. He paid a price for his courage. The police department set out to systematically discredit the young writer. They ransacked his rooms and then spread rumors that he was a degenerate, a dope addict and even a Satanist! Unable to stand this harassment, Crane again fled New York. Years later, Charles Becker was convicted in a murder case and went to the electric chair.

Crane's restless spirit now took him south, by train, to Jacksonville, Florida. A New York newspaper hired him to report on the growing turmoil in Cuba. The Cuban people were in revolt against the Spanish, who had controlled the island for over four centuries. Although U.S. support was unofficial, sympathetic Americans were sending shiploads of rifles and ammunition to help the Cubans. Crane was eager to see the fighting firsthand and, if possible verify the authenticity of his *Red Badge* battle descriptions.

On December 31, 1896, disguised as a crew member, Crane left Florida on a tugboat. Once out at sea, the ship's boiler exploded. A few men died in the explosion, the rest abandoned ship in small lifeboats. For 30 hours, Crane and the other survivors floated helplessly without food or fresh water before washing up on the Florida coast. It was a terrible ordeal that the writer transformed into one of his finest stories, "The Open Boat."

The Cuban expedition was a failure, but while in Florida, Crane met a captivating woman, Cora Taylor. Two years older than Crane, Cora had been married twice before. Together, they set off for Greece to report on the impending war between Greece and Turkey. Under the name "Imogene Carter," Cora would also send home dispatches as the first woman war correspondent for an American newspaper.

Once again, Crane was disappointed in his attempt to experience a real war. The guerrilla war he observed had none of the drama or excitement he envisioned. His health suffering from years of neglect, Crane was constantly sick and found himself unable to write even a good war dispatch. After several months, he moved with Cora to England, where they set up housekeeping in a villa.

In the quiet English countryside, Crane soon regained his energy and inspiration. He turned out dozens of short stories, including some of his very best. Two Western stories, "The Blue Hotel" and "The Bride Comes to Yellow Sky," were based on people and places he had glimpsed on a trip West years earlier. In England, he formed meaningful, lasting friendships with such great writers as Joseph Conrad, H. G. Wells and another American living abroad, Henry James.

But once more, action and adventure beckoned. The U.S. battleship *Maine* was mysteriously sunk in Cuba's Havana harbor, and many Americans accused the Spanish of sabotage. The result was the Spanish-American War, one of the briefest conflicts the U.S. was ever involved in.

Anxious not to miss out on another opportunity to see men in combat, Crane returned to New York and tried to enlist, but was rejected as physically unfit. He was hired at once by the *New York World* as a correspondent, and left for Key West, Florida. After much waiting, he joined American marines in the invasion of Cuba's Guantanamo Bay. Like Henry Fleming, Crane was determined to test himself in the heat of battle, and bravely faced death and hardship along with the common soldiers for four days and nights. He soon caught yellow fever, a deadly infectious disease, but refused to leave the country. He stayed on, writing doggedly, after the war ended in an American victory.

When Crane finally returned to New York, he was a physical wreck. To worsen matters, the New York police, not forgetting his attack on their reputation, hounded and harrassed him. He returned to England and Cora in January, 1899.

They moved into a 600-year-old manor, but the peace that the writer sought continued to elude him. Hopelessly in debt and pestered by unwanted visitors, Crane wrote frantically, turning out a new story every couple of days. Many of them were so bad that he was afraid to read them over, for fear of tearing them up before he could sell them. He had been diagnosed as having tuberculosis in Cuba, and he knew his days were numbered.

On May 15, 1900, Cora, in desperation, had him taken to a sanatorium in Badenweiler, Germany, near the Swiss border. After a tortuous two-week journey, they arrived at the hospital. There, on June 5, Stephen Crane died in a second-floor room. He was just five months shy of his 29th birthday.

Stephen Crane's short life was one of constant struggle. Considering this, the high quality of much of his writing seems all the more incredible. His best work captures the reality of life as no American writer had before. But Crane was much more than a mere recorder of reality. He was a true artist. His colorful descriptions of landscapes and characters bring them vividly to life. He also infused his writing with a subtle symbolism that heightened its power.

If he had lived longer, this last great American writer of the 19th century may have been the first great writer of the 20th century.

Still, Crane was a major influence on such modern American masters as Ernest Hemingway and Norman Mailer, both of whom wrote about men in action with grace and gritty realism. Out of rebellion, Stephen Crane, the rebel writer, created a new tradition in American literature.

Chronology

November 1, 1871   born in Newark, New Jersey

1890   attends Syracuse University for one semester

1891   moves to New York City to work as free-lance journalist

1892   *Maggie: A Girl of the Streets* published

1895   *The Red Badge of Courage* and *The Black Riders*, a collection of poems, published

1896–97   attempts to reach Cuba to cover revolution but ship sinks; uses harrowing experience in "The Open Boat"

1897   travels to Greece to cover the Greco-Turkish War; settles in Surrey, England with companion, Cora Taylor

1898   serves as war correspondent in Cuba during Spanish-American War

1899   returns to England and lives with Cora in old manor

June 5, 1900   dies of tuberculosis in Badenweiler, Germany

Further Reading

Crane's Works

Maggie and Other Stories (New York: Washington Square Press, paper, 1960). A good anthology, including Crane's first novel and 15 stories, some of them his best.

The Open Boat and Other Stories (New York: Scholastic, 1968, paper). This collection, specially prepared for young adults, includes several examples of Crane's unique poetry.

The Red Badge of Courage (New York: Macmillan, 1967). A good young-adult edition of Crane's masterpiece, well illustrated by Herschel Levit and with an afterword by Clifton Fadiman.

Books About Stephen Crane

Ruth Franchere, *Stephen Crane: the story of an American writer* (New York: Thomas Crowell, 1961). Partly fictionalized, but a well-researched and clearly written young-adult biography.

Index

Bold numbers indicate main headings;
italic numbers indicate illustrations

Index

Index

Index

Index